SUCCEEDING IN THE WORKPLACE...

CRITICAL SKILLS FOR A REWARDING CAREER

AND LIFE YOU LOVE

By SUSAN E. RACE

A PERSONAL GROWTH SYSTEMS PUBLICATION
YARDLEY, PENNSYLVANIA 19067 - 6378
http://www.personalgrowthsystems.com

SUCCEEDING IN THE WORKPLACE...
CRITICAL SKILLS FOR A REWARDING CAREER AND LIFE YOU LOVE
by SUSAN E. RACE

A PERSONAL GROWTH SYSTEMS Publication
Printed in the United States of America

ISBN 0-9673542-7-7

Credits:
Book Design: Jason Greene
Cover Design: Jason Greene
Editor: Mary Beth Regan
Illustrations: Jason Greene
Logo: Mary Katz
Photo (Back Cover) Howard Karashoff

To my mother and best friend, Harriet

ACKNOWLEDGEMENTS

My sincere appreciation and gratitude go to those who have helped in completing this book. In particular, my immediate family who, throughout my life, believed in my dreams and told me I could be and do anything I want, as long as I had a plan. I am grateful to my illustrator and designer, Jason Greene whose vivid imagination, talent and hard work made these pages come alive. My editor and long-time friend, Mary Beth Regan shared her levelheaded perspective to help me through many trying times in the workplace and life. My friends, Dr. Gary M. Glass, Dr. Louis Esparo, Patty Szostak, Patricia A. McDade, Peter Panthauer, Linda Simmons and Bonnie LaRoche showed me what successful relationships are all about. My colleagues, John Sosinski, John Zick, Bill Yanavitch, Dr. Carolyn Primus, and James M. Mandell created learning experiences in the workplace that are sprinkled throughout these pages. My husband George patiently stood by me and made me laugh through many months of writing and building a business. Fellow writers and friends, Phil Bruschi and Jim Donovan provided moral support and suggestions for assembling and distributing this book. My coach, Michael Stratford helped me focus throughout this experience.
Thanks to all my clients who believe in my talents and allow me to practice my skill as coach, trainer, and professional speaker.
Lastly, I acknowledge authors and leaders Warren Bennis, Brian Tracy, Wayne Dyer and Tony Robbins whose audio tape cassettes and books inspired me to grow my dreams, spread my wings and S O A R!

INTRODUCTION

What do you want to be when you grow up? The age-old question that challenges people from age 5 through 65. Ask anyone working today how much their education prepared them for the workplace and you'll hear, "Not much." Ask any student today what help he or she would like with their career, and you'll hear, "I don't know what I want to do, and how will things I learned in school help me at work?"

Throughout my 20 years experience in Human Resources management, I was amazed at how long it took to find qualified candidates and how poorly prepared many of them were for the workplace. Even when we were able to hire people whom we believed would perform effectively, there were endless issues with personality conflicts, lack of motivation, or inability to adapt to the business environment. The biggest challenge facing businesses today is still finding, attracting, and retaining competent workers and leaders.

Like me, most people that I worked with and meet today said that everything they learned about succeeding in the workplace and life came from on-the-job experience. Few believe that they were told what to expect about the company or properly trained to perform their jobs. Most people follow their instincts and fly by the seat of their pants. Unfortunately, this often results in poor performance, interpersonal conflicts, and low self-esteem.

I recognized that businesses could create a better workforce by partnering with educators to prepare students for the workplace. This would help businesses grow while helping students become responsible citizens who build rewarding lives. School-to-Work partnerships sprung up in the early 1990's, teaming businesses with educators. Together they arrange work experiences for students while still attending school.

This early exposure to the business world helps many students decide which field they would like to pursue and provides experiences that help them gain employment after graduation.

The world of work is changing constantly. The best opportunities for employment are those that you create for yourself based on your interests and talents. Whether you go it alone straight from school or at any point during your career, the experience that you gain from working in an established business will be invaluable to you throughout your life.

There's an expression that says, 'forewarned is forearmed'. This means that knowing what you are about to face helps you prepare yourself for whatever challenges you may encounter. The only person that you can control is yourself. By arming yourself with the knowledge and strategies in this book, you will be prepared for the situations that you'll encounter in the workplace and life.

Anticipate them and practice how you want to respond when you face them. This preparation will lead to your success in all aspects of life.

Though just a piece of your life, work does occupy a major part of your time and requires your full attention. Working gives you the resources to create the kind of life that you desire.

Regardless of which career you choose, or where you become employed, the skills covered in this book will help you communicate effectively, think rationally, and build the relationships that you'll need throughout your life. As a result, you will gain the confidence, self-esteem and skills necessary to explore new opportunities and welcome your just rewards each step along the way.

You may choose to read this book from front to back, or turn to any page and browse. Chapter 1 encourages you to do what you want to do versus what others want for you. Chapter 2 tells you what business is about and the types that exist. Chapters 3 – 10 concentrate on specific skills necessary to succeed in the workplace and life. Chapter 11 addresses interviewing and Chapter 12 recaps the highlights from the prior chapters.
In between, you'll find entertaining illustrations to reinforce the main points in each chapter.

Relax and enjoy your journey. Let me know where you wind up and how I can help you continue succeeding in the workplace and life!

TABLE OF CONTENTS

- CHAPTER 1 -

The Choice is Yours!
What do you want to do?

Get ready to Soar!

"What do you want to be when you grow up?" The question we hear from age 5 to 65...

The answer is: *You can be and do anything you want, as long as you have a plan and remain flexible* ☺

Life is what you make it. Your career is just one piece of your life. It's the work *you choose* to do so you can have the things and live the kind of life that you want. You may even choose to change your career several times in your lifetime.

Change is one thing that you can depend on happening throughout your career and life. Change is normal and is often valuable. Change just for the sake of change can be counterproductive to what you want to achieve. Welcome each change and choice you make as a learning experience and chance to grow.

CHOOSING CAREERS

Selecting your career is the beginning of building the quality of life that's rewarding to *you*. Think about planning your career as giving yourself a present. It will bring you the rewards that you desire now and later. If you simply wait to see what happens without any planning, you risk becoming a victim of circumstance rather than a winner by choice.

Your career consists of your:

1. **Jobs** – the roles you play and work you perform for an employer.
2. **Goals** – what you want to accomplish

3

3. **Relationships** – the people you meet and work with
4. **Competencies** – the skills, knowledge and abilities that you bring to, use or develop while performing jobs and building your career.

You *will succeed in the workplace* and life when you understand yourself, know what you want and commit to doing whatever it takes to get it.

Follow this systematic process to increase your likelihood for success:

- Assess your interests, skills, abilities, and aptitudes
- Develop a 'can do' attitude
- Explore jobs associated with different fields or professions
- Dare to dream
- Determine your motivation to proceed
- Draft a plan to achieve your dream, and
- Commit to doing *whatever* it takes, legally and ethically, to accomplish your goal.
- Follow your plan!

Knowing your interests is the first step to choosing your career.

INTERESTS

To determine your interests, list the things that you think about often, would choose to do before anything else, and make you feel good just thinking about them.

Ask people who know you well what *they* think interests you. They'll name things that you talk about non-stop, that make you laugh, give you lots of energy and occupy your time.

Your interests are the things that grab your attention. Sometimes just watching somebody do something or hearing about someone else's hobby or work sparks your interest. Other times, you know something interests you because you're always daydreaming about it and look forward to time when you can pursue it.

Which of these grabs your attention?

- Sports [playing or observing]
- Music [listening, playing an instrument, or singing]
- Cooking
- Reading
- Art
- Writing
- Computers
- Gardening
- Operating machinery
- Boating
- Building furniture or woodwork
- Riding a bicycle or motor bike
- Solving crossword puzzles
- Constructing jigsaw puzzles
- Solving brainteasers or mathematical problems
- Theater or movies
- Acting
- Traveling
- Camping
- Hiking

Which ones do you want to do soon? Those are your interests. What do you like that isn't listed here? How do you feel when you think about or devote time to that interest?

In which school subjects do you earn good grades or are you motivated to study– science, math, history, English, a foreign language, art, health, business, psychology, sociology? What jobs have you held that you enjoy doing and are praised for your results? Once you know what interests you, determine how motivated you are to pursue these activities.
The more time you devote to an interest, the stronger it is.

Maybe your interest is art. Do you like all art or a specialty like sculpting, painting, drawing or ceramics? How often do you work on a piece to develop your skill? What else do you do to explore this interest? How do you like your results? What could you do differently to produce results that you like even more? What do other people say about your work?

Devoting time to an interest helps you develop it into a skill. When you do work that interests you, you perform better.

Employers hire employees who are skilled in performing tasks that the jobs in their company require. When you do what you love, your work is better quality, you stay focused more easily and you are more likely to succeed.

FINDING YOUR PASSION

Succeeding in the workplace, whether working for someone else or your own business, depends on doing something that you love. Doing what you love is a combination of applying your interests and skills.

Thomas J. Stanley, author of <u>The Millionaire Next Door,</u> told Entrepreneur Magazine that, "Anyone with a reasonable income can become financially independent in a lifetime. Do something you love. It's the feeling that *this* is what I should be doing; it's not just for the money."

Something in which you are both interested and skilled is your strength. Recognizing your strengths is a key point in determining what you would like to build your career around and what types of jobs you will seek.

You are dynamic! Human beings have a curious nature and look for challenging, exciting opportunities. Choose ones that interest you, allow you to apply your strengths and learn new skills. This will help you grow, personally and professionally.

Employers favorably consider employees with many skills and abilities when promotional opportunities or special projects arise. The more you know and the more you're willing to learn, the more valuable you are to your employer. Thus, the more you will enjoy your work and your life.

Some people know intuitively what they would like to do and believe they'd be good at. They seem to have a 'calling' to pursue a particular career or field. Others are not as sure.

If you don't know what you'd like to do, research the jobs that relate to your hobbies and interests. Wouldn't it be great if you could make a lot of money playing computer games? People who work for Blizzard Entertainment, ID Software and Lucas Arts get to do that every day ☺

Somebody's got to invent and test those games before they get to the market. Bill Gates, the richest man in the world, built his empire on something he did for a hobby. Even if you think you know what you want to do, speak to people who are currently in that line of work to help you decide if it's what you really want to do.

Career decisions can occur early in life!

What did you say when you were a little child and people asked you, "What do you want to be when you grow up?" Some people know very early in life what they want to be. Young children are very creative because they haven't learned to fear failure and won't hold back their thoughts for fear of sounding foolish. Ask a young child today what he or she wants to be when he or she grows up, and you may hear – computer programmer, webmaster, astronaut, doctor, lawyer, teacher, firefighter, nurse, actor/actress, dancer, artist, policeman, magician, professional athlete, etc. You never can tell with kids. Jeremy Epstein, a 7 – year old guest on television's <u>Kids Say the Darndest Things</u>, told Bill Cosby that when he grows up he plans to be "…a mind reader and partner of Bill Gates".

At age three and one half years old, Zachary Garfinkel declared that he intends to be a paleontologist. Fascinated by dinosaurs, he collects them, reads about them and is drawn to games, programs and stories about them. Still in grade school, Zachary is on his way to developing a career from an interest.

Sara Savini, a 15 – year old in Yardley, Pennsylvania is an accomplished playwright and producer. Sara wrote a play, composed the music, assembled the cast and used her own savings to pay for the props, costumes, and theater rental. She plans to continue writing throughout high school and college.

I announced at five years old that I was going to be a teacher when I grew up. Friends who didn't know what they wanted to do ridiculed me for being so certain. Their comments hurt and I questioned whether something was wrong with me for knowing what I wanted to do. My parents always told me that I was responsible for my own choices and could do and be whatever I wanted.

I stayed true to my goal. Immediately upon earning my Bachelors degree in Education and Psychology, I found a teaching job. After earning my Masters degree in Human Behavior and Development, I sought jobs in business. The training and development function was emerging in the Human Resources department – teaching employees skills necessary to perform their jobs effectively and contribute to their company's success. I was able to continue my love for teaching while expanding my skills and abilities in the field of human resources.

All of my jobs have involved teaching, coaching and helping others to succeed and achieve their personal best. By choosing paths consistent with my interests and goals, I found and continue to find opportunities that bring rewards, monetarily and psychologically.

When you find your purpose, you will discover opportunities to practice and apply your skills.

Remember that *you can do and be anything you want, as long as you have a plan and remain flexible* ☺

Stay true to your own beliefs rather than let others' fears or insecurities dissuade you from following your dream.

Successful people will tell you, "The world steps aside for a person who knows where he or she is headed."

In his book, The Celestine Prophecy, James Redfield tells us to be aware of the people and events that come into our lives. Redfield believes that nothing in life is a 'coincidence' or 'accident'. You never know when you'll meet someone who may know of a job that interests you. Remaining open-minded to the possibility of this occurring will present you with ideal opportunities on your journey through life.

Jason M. Greene, who illustrated this book, is passionate about computers and graphic art. He initially wanted to pursue a career in cinematography, creating special effects for directors like George Lucas and Steven Spielberg. When he enrolled at the University of Maryland, there were no majors designed for this career. Jason created his own major combining studio art and computer technology.

He attended a 'Sesame Street' exhibit at the University which was scheduled for the Smithsonian Institute in Washington DC. Jason observed a problem with Big Bird and suggested how to fix it. Jane Henson rewarded him with a job at the Henson Studios in New York the following summer.

Jason's interests in art and computers grow in different directions. He continues to develop and expand his skills, looking for opportunities to apply his talent. About to enter his senior year, Jason has his own web design business called Wookie Works, Inc. With more business than he can handle, he hired five employees. He also designed a logo for clothing. Through networking, Jason found a clothing manufacturer that will release his logo this Fall. He has joined partners with other businesses in New York that utilize his computer design skills for lucrative returns.

Knowing his purpose helps Jason seek opportunities and make wise choices about those he finds. Staying focused leads him on paths to discover what is available to help him. By doing what he loves, Jason continues to receive offers to expand his business, and is meeting the people he needs to pursue his dreams.

YOU *can* do this too!

If you love science, you might consider a career in biotechnology, aerospace, engineering or environmental research. If you are good in math and enjoy working with numbers, you'll probably be interested in jobs in finance, accounting and technology. If you have a penchant for cooking, you might explore jobs in hotel and restaurant management or catering, nutritional research or food photography. If you're a whiz on the computer, start looking at existing jobs in the computer industry and then imagine applications that no one has thought of yet.

If you are fascinated by cars, consider jobs in the automobile industry, at racetracks or as an auto mechanic. If you have artistic talents, you might consider jobs designing clothing, home decor or jewelry, interior decorating or architecture. If you are particularly expressive and enjoy acting, you can explore opportunities in the entertainment field. You get the picture. The list is endless.

Articles in newspapers and business magazines indicate that **opportunities for skilled workers are greatest in the healthcare, insurance and high-tech industries.** The future holds infinite opportunities for people who want to work for a company or start their own business.

To succeed on your own, it helps to first work for an established company to learn the basics of running a business, develop your interpersonal communication and team building skills, and develop a network of resources.

Where can you find information to help you in making wise choices?

Available Resources

You've assessed your interests, skills and abilities and want to learn about the various professions available. Where can you start? Several resources are available to help you with your research:

1. **Career Days** at school and community organizations feature panels of professionals who talk about their jobs and what they did to get where they are.

2. **Personal Contacts** – parents, relatives, neighbors and many others in your community are willing to talk to you about their work. Talk to your doctor, dentist, clergy, family accountant or attorney, local baker, restaurant and retail store owners, plumbers, builders, bankers, auto mechanics, police and teachers.

Ask them what they do, how they got their current job, what they like or don't like as well. [In order for you to make an informed choice, you need to know it all – the good, the bad, and the ugly!]

12

3. **The library** reference and periodical sections, stacks of business books and public bookstores are excellent sources for information about careers and industries.
Ask your librarian for the <u>Dictionary of Occupational Titles</u> <u>[DOT]</u> produced and updated frequently by the U.S. Department of Labor. This book contains abstracts of various positions, the anticipated salary range and the requirements necessary to obtain each job.

4. **Business people** in your area are often willing to meet with you for an *Informational Interview*. Request about 20 minutes for a brief discussion with someone who is currently performing a job that you'd like to know more about. Your interview will help you determine if it interests you. Ask the person you interview to tell you how they got their job, what they like about it, what they see as some of the challenges in it, and what you should do if you'd like to pursue a career in their field or industry. If you approach these people politely and confidently, they *may* help you find a job or hire you.

5. **Internet** databases abound for job opportunities. If you don't have a computer or access to the Internet, they're often available in libraries, major bookstores, computer stores, or businesses in your community.

6. **The media** is another source for jobs. Newspapers, magazines, television and radio news and other programs, books you read and the movies you see all feature people who perform jobs that you may want to explore. Relying on the employment classifieds, however, is the least likely way for you to grow your career. You will discover more opportunities through a process called networking, which is covered in chapter 10.

7. **Schools** – personnel at technical trade schools, colleges, universities, and independent personal-development schools throughout the country are more than happy to talk to you or provide literature about their programs. Most are willing to help you draft your curriculum and tell you how to finance your education with them.

Take the initiative to approach people and obtain the resources available to get the information you need to choose a career that's right for you. To use your resources effectively, have a clear idea of what you're looking for. If you need help, look in the Yellow Pages or ask your friends for the name of a career coach in your area.

In his book, <u>The Aladdin Factor</u>, Mark Victor Hansen demonstrates the rewards associated with asking others for the help you need. Even the Bible says, "Seek and Ye shall Find". The worst that can happen when you ask someone for help is they'll say no. So what? You're no further behind than you were before asking, and there's a greater likelihood that they'll say yes.

Information about jobs is usually organized by industry. Traditional industries include:

❖ agriculture, forestry and fishing
❖ mining
❖ construction
❖ manufacturing
❖ transportation, and public utilities [gas, electric and telephone]
❖ aerospace
❖ finance, insurance and real estate
❖ education

- entertainment
- public administration/government
- retail trade
- service, and
- Non-classified businesses.

Jennifer James, author of <u>Thinking in the Future Tense</u>, suggests that more jobs in the future will be contained within these newly emerging industries:

- Fiber optics – Use of light beams to transport information through glass fibers finer than a human hair
- Photonics – Using networks of telephones to link computers and provide instant data, worldwide
- Space colonization – Solar satellites, the new frontier of asteroid mining and untapped sources for living
- Alternative energy – Exploring the use of ethanol, methanol, compressed natural gas, liquid hydrogen and propane for fuels
- Nanotechnology – A process to build everything [homes, cars, food and computers] out of individual atoms
- Lasers – Computer-guided beams used for manufacturing, surgery and dentistry
- Genetics – Engineering food, drugs, body parts and processes to eliminate congenital defects and inherited diseases.

Once you have an idea of the jobs that interest you, define what *success* means to *you*. Unless you know what success is, how will you know when you've made it?

DEFINING SUCCESS

Success means different things to different people. For some it's money. For others it's recognition and for still others, success means helping people less fortunate than they. Research shows that most people only enjoy the visible signs of success for brief periods of time. Successful people say that success comes from achieving worthwhile goals, from helping others, and from believing they've made a difference.

What works for others may not necessarily work for you. When you've defined what success means to you, draft concrete, measurable goals that you want to achieve. Goals are discussed in detail in chapter 6 on Planning and Organizing.

Knowing what success means to you also helps you determine how motivated you are to exert the effort to achieve your goals.

MOTIVATION

Motivation is the urge to act. Anything that in*spires* you to take action is a motivator. All human beings are motivated by two strong emotions – **pleasure** and **pain**. You are drawn towards anything that you believe will bring you pleasure. It motivates you to exert the effort to achieve or obtain it.

In contrast, you move away from anything painful or that has the potential to cause you pain in the future. It motivates you to act to eliminate or avoid the pain.

For example, the following are likely to bring you pleasure:

❖ Finishing a report before it is due gives you time to work on other things or pursue your interests

❖ Being appointed captain of the team or earning a promotion at work brings you recognition
❖ Receiving a desirable job offer brings you relief in knowing that you will be earning a living to cover your needs.
❖ Rock climbing can be an exhilarating activity that elevates your adrenaline and brings physical pleasure.
❖ Taking a trip or attending an event with your friends satisfies your need to feel included, knowing that you belong.
❖ Earning good grades inspires pride in your intelligence and can mean acceptance into the school of your choice.
❖ Landing the lead role in a play can be fun as well as generate opportunities in the theater.

What brings *YOU* pleasure? How would your life improve if you looked for opportunities to increase these pleasures?

The following are examples of pain that you may currently feel and want to eliminate or believe have the potential to bring you pain and thus you want to avoid:

❖ *Embarrassment* when people ridicule you for a bad habit.
❖ *Isolation* from having few friends or not being invited to join the crowd for an event.
❖ *Shame* for failing a course because you didn't study enough.
❖ *Regret* about missing the concert because you waited too long to buy tickets.
❖ *Low self-esteem* because you continuously doubt your abilities and thus refuse to try something new.
❖ *Lack of confidence* because you don't understand or know how to do something and are reluctant to ask for help or clarification.

What else brings *YOU* pain? How are you holding yourself
back from being all that you are capable of?

We are all motivated to satisfy basic needs, wants, and desires.
Behavioral scientist, Abraham Maslow, defined these needs
and the order in which they must be satisfied. He categorized
these needs in ascending order of development from survival to
spiritual:

1. Basic needs – food, clothing, and shelter
2. Security or Safety – to be protected from danger
3. Social – need to belong, to be loved, accepted and
    respected by others
4. Ego protection – self esteem, pride, status and
    recognition
5. Self-actualization – realizing our fullest potential and
    becoming all we can become.

Needs at one level must be satisfied before you can address
those at the next level. Once satisfied, a need is no longer a
motivator. It becomes a need again if the satisfiers disappear.
For example, when you need a home, you focus on finding a
suitable dwelling. If your home is damaged by fire, or you
outgrow the space you're in, you are once again motivated to
find a new home.

The primary reason people work is to earn money to satisfy
their basic survival needs. Everyone needs food, clothing, a
home safe from the elements and medical care from time to
time. You need money to buy the goods and services necessary
for these basic needs of survival. Unless you inherit a fortune,
you'll have to work for the money you need. How much money
you need depends on your values and the lifestyle that you
choose to achieve and maintain.

People work for reasons in addition to earning money.

These reasons include:
- ❖ Desire to learn new skills
- ❖ Opportunity to conduct research in a particular field
- ❖ Desire to perform a service that will enrich the world for others.

Working with others can satisfy some of your social needs. If you have a strong need to make a difference in the world, you may choose to work in a social services business that provides goods and services to improve people's health or lifestyle. Even if you prefer to spend most of your time alone, you'll need to interact with other people. We all want to feel important and be with others to some degree.

Your *need* for love and acceptance should be satisfied from friends, family and contacts **outside** the workplace. If you do develop a romantic attachment at work, be discreet so as not to give the impression that you're more interested in your love life than you are in doing your job well.

Looking for romance in the workplace diverts your attention from your job and is likely to have a negative impact on your performance.

Your motivation to satisfy your needs will determine which career you pursue. Once you're working, do what the job requires to achieve the business' objectives. Look for factors in your job that motivate you to accomplish what must be done. If you are no longer motivated to perform well in your job, you owe it to yourself and your employer to seek employment elsewhere.

19

Motivators are things that you want. *Wanting* something is good if it inspires you to act. Getting it requires your commitment of exerting the effort to achieve the desired results. Motivation is your internal driving force to act to attain the motivator.

Once you know *what* you're motivated to achieve, HOW can you achieve it? Suppose that you want to:

❖ **Be selected for or assigned to a specific project or team**

Ask the team leader what you must do to earn a place on the team or to be assigned the role that you want.

❖ **Achieve a certain grade in a course**
Spend more time studying difficult subjects or ask a tutor to help you grasp what you don't understand.

❖ **Land the leading part in a play**
Ask the director how he or she will select the players. Then practice/rehearse the lines to the play until you're comfortable that you can perform in a manner that convinces the director that you're the best person for that role.

❖ **Have enough money to buy a car**
Look at what you currently spend your money on, and determine how you can cut back or eliminate things you can do without. OR, determine what you can do at work to earn extra money.

Whenever you are motivated to do something, your mind thinks of ways to achieve the result. Focus on the end result [the pleasure], not the process it will take to get there [sometimes considered the pain]. Focusing on the actual goal stimulates your brain to determine how to get there. Andre Agassi repeatedly envisioned himself winning an award at Wimbledon before he actually received it. By focusing on the reward, his mind instructed his body on how to play to beat his competition.

If what you want requires money, determine how much you'll need and how long you'll have to work to earn the desired object.

If you're working full-time, draft a budget to cover your fixed expenses like rent, car payments, food and utilities, and insurance. Establish a savings plan to accrue the money you need for your additional wants.

If you're still in school or not earning what you need in your current job, your mind will look for ways to generate the money you need. You could generate money from a part–time job or starting your own service business.

Part – time jobs are available at schools, in restaurants, hospitals, businesses or retail stores. Companies often need employees who can work part – time in the afternoons, evenings, or on weekends to do light assembly, cleaning, telemarketing, typing, or customer service work. The kind of work you look for and obtain will depend on your skills, abilities and interests as well as the time available to work while attending to your other activities and responsibilities. If you can't find a job that you want advertised in the papers, create your own business by offering services that other people are willing to pay you to do. Family, friends and neighbors will often pay you to do chores for them.

Think of the things that you and your family do every day. Other people do and need the same things and are often willing to pay you to do these things for them. People are motivated to pay for services and items that will save them time and give them the freedom to pursue their own interests and activities.

Chores that people are willing to pay you for include:

- Babysitting
- Cooking and serving meals
- Shoveling snow
- Gardening and landscaping
- Walking dogs
- Grooming horses
- Cleaning houses
- Painting houses or fences
- Re-surfacing driveways
- Cleaning/washing or ironing clothes
- Running errands to the grocery store

The list is endless.

Twenty-five year old Bennett Holmes of Rye Beach, New Hampshire built a very successful landscaping business from a hobby that began when he was 12.

Ben started mowing neighbors' lawns during the summer to earn some money. He grew fascinated in the process and selected the University of Vermont to pursue a degree in Urban Forestry and Landscape Horticulture.

Ben expanded his business during college and immediately upon graduation became the full-time owner/operator of Rye Beach Landscaping. Today he employs 5 people and has the equipment he needs to run a full-service landscaping and snow-removal business.

Ben told me that his largest contract last year was for $50,000 to completely install a lawn for a new house. That was just one of many.

He and his staff currently maintain 65 lawns every week. Other services include full landscape construction, lawn, plant and tree installations, and some stone work. Ben says he doesn't have to do much marketing. The quality of his work speaks for itself and he is constantly receiving new business from word-of-mouth referrals.
If you'd like to know how Ben created his business, you can reach him at (603) 964-6888.

What hobby can *you* turn into a successful service business? Whether you work for someone else, or start your own business, you're more likely to succeed in work and life when you are motivated to excel.

When your *wants* and needs exceed your income, you'll be motivated to earn additional money. You can do this by:

❖ Looking for ways to generate profits for your employer and ask for a raise.

❖ Earning a merit increase in your current job [Employees are usually eligible for a merit increase every year on the anniversary of their date of hire. Being eligible does not mean that you will automatically receive one if your performance doesn't meet expectations and doesn't warrant a merit increase.]

❖ Increasing your skills so you are more valuable to your present employer and prospective employers,

❖ Working a second job

❖ Exploring means of increasing your income through savings and wise investments.

What motivates you to *do* something? You can only motivate yourself. What somebody else says or does may inspire you, but nobody else can motivate you. Doing things for your reasons rather than other people's reasons increases the likelihood of your success.

For example, when your parents tell you it's time to study, your initial reaction is likely to resist what they tell you to do. When you choose to study because *you* want to learn a particular subject or earn a certain grade, you do it without anyone reminding you that you need to. You may resist an assignment that your boss delegates to you, but wanting to keep your job and earn your paycheck will motivate you to accept it

Doing something that someone else suggests is a good way for you to try new activities to determine if they interest you. And trying new activities is a good way to expand your talents and abilities, as well as build rewarding relationships. In the end, the reason you take action is because you decide something is worth doing.

Kim Kivler is a good example of what happens when you do what *others* want you to do rather than the things that *you* choose to do. Kim enrolled in Kutztown University to become a teacher because her parents wanted her to.

During her first two years, Kim was miserable, gained weight and lost her motivation to study. Embarrassed, feeling she had 'wasted' her parents' money and her time pursuing a path she didn't like, Kim didn't know how to tell her parents that she wanted to quit school. She finally found her courage and admitted that she was studying to be a teacher because they wanted her to, but her heart wasn't in it.

Her mom asked Kim what her plan was. She didn't have one and didn't know what she wanted to do. Her mother suggested a career coach to help Kim develop a plan. Kim feared that her parents would disapprove of the career that appealed to her.

When her mother asked her what she really wanted to do, Kim replied, "If I told you, Daddy would be terribly disappointed in me." When her mother urged her to speak her mind, Kim revealed that she wanted to be a cosmetologist.

Her mother thought this was a great idea and asked Kim, "What do you think about finding a good trade school for cosmetology, and transfer your two years of college credits to an evening school where you can finish your degree in business?" This would prepare Kim to run her own beauty salon one day.

Kim was thrilled with the idea. She had a plan that motivated her to take action and that her father fully supported.

Kim regained her confidence, lost the excess weight, and is happier than she had been during her early years in college. She is employed in a salon, learning all the aspects of running a beauty business and is engaged to a man who is self-employed. They plan to be independent business owners pursuing their dreams of rewarding careers and lives that they love.

As you mature and progress in your career, your desire to satisfy the fifth level of human needs – self-actualization – becomes stronger. The need for self-actualization is often satisfied in the workplace.

Doing work that you find rewarding and meaningful develops self-confidence, self-respect, and deep pride in your accomplishments. Work that you enjoy has the highest likelihood of meeting all of your needs, from basic through spiritual.

Knowing what motivates you will help you select a career path in an industry that affords you opportunities for success, growth and development. The next chapter will help you understand the business world.

Life is what you make it! Grow your dreams, spread your wings, and S O A R [Seize Opportunity And Rewards!]

TIPS TO S O A R [Seize Opportunity And Rewards!]

❖ You can do and be anything you want, as long as you have a plan and remain flexible.

❖ You *will succeed in the workplace* and life when you understand yourself, know what you want and commit to doing whatever it takes to get it.

❖ A systematic process will increase your likelihood for success: Assess your interests, skills, abilities, and aptitudes. Have a 'can do' attitude, Explore different fields, Dare to dream, Commit to doing *whatever* it takes, legally and ethically, to accomplish your goal. Draft and follow a plan to achieve your dream.

❖ Succeeding in the workplace, whether working for someone else or in your own business, depends on doing something that you love.

❖ Employers hire employees who are skilled in performing tasks that are required by certain jobs.

❖ When you find your purpose, you will discover opportunities to practice and apply your skills.

❖ To succeed on your own, first work for an established company to learn the basics of running a business and develop your skills.

❖ Knowing what success means to you also helps you determine how motivated you are to exert the effort to achieve your goals.

Which tips from chapter 1 do *you* value most?
List them below:

Pave your own road...

- CHAPTER 2 -

Minding Your Business

Businesses come in all shapes and sizes...

The purpose of business is to make money.

TYPES OF BUSINESS: The dictionary defines business as:

1. Profit-seeking enterprise or concern.
2. The purchase and sale of goods in an attempt to make a profit.
3. A person, partnership, or corporation engaged in commerce, manufacturing, or a service.

For tax purposes, businesses are classified as either 'For Profit' or 'Non-Profit'. Each has a unique structure and offers you various opportunities.

The money a company receives for selling its goods and/or services is called *income or revenue.* The money a company spends to produce or provide their goods and services is called *expenses.*

A Company makes a <u>profit</u> when income exceeds expenses.

Profit is often referred to as *the bottom line* because it's reported on the last line at the bottom of the page of a business' financial report. Profit is also referred to as 'positive drop through' because it results in plus balances on the bottom line as opposed to negative deficits.

Many of the companies that you know are 'for – profit' businesses. They *manufacture* and sell goods or products to the general public to make a profit.

For - Profit Businesses

Some of the 'for profit' businesses you are familiar with include
General Motors, L.L. Bean, Microsoft, and Pepsi Co.
The goods they sell include:

- ❖ Automobiles
- ❖ Clothing
- ❖ Computer programs
- ❖ Food

You can buy their products in stores, through catalogs, or from
a salesperson.

Other 'for-profit' businesses sell *services*. Some of these
companies include Aetna/US Healthcare, Metropolitan Life,
First Union Bank, American Telephone and Telegraph
(AT&T), and Choice Hotels. Their services include:

- ❖ Insurance policies and medical benefits,
- ❖ Loans, checking or savings accounts
- ❖ Telephone, fax, paging and internet connections
- ❖ Lodging

Although Service companies call their services 'products', you
can't see or touch them like you can the products from a
company that sells manufactured goods like beverages,
clothing, cars, or computers.

Companies use various methods to generate income.
Most often, they sell their goods or services to customers.
To sell their products, a company may use one, all, or a
combination of the following:

- ❖ **Direct sales** [Company employees initiate contact with and call on customers in person or on the telephone]

- ❖ **Catalogue Sales** [Company distributes catalogues featuring their products to customers through the mail – customers place orders through return mail or by calling the Company]

- ❖ **Dealers, Distributor, or Brokers** [independent companies that charge a fee to sell or distribute another company's goods]

- ❖ **Trade shows** [several companies in the same industry meet in a large convention hall on a set date to display their goods/services to customers who visit the event]

Businesses also generate revenue through selling shares of stock. Private investors purchase stock through stockbrokers. Employees purchase ore receive stock through Company Pension plans.

Businesses use their income to pay their operating expenses. These include:

- ❖ Employees' salaries and benefits
- ❖ Rent for office space, manufacturing plants and/or distribution centers
- ❖ Equipment and office furniture [machinery, computers, copiers, desks, fax machines, file cabinets, etc.]
- ❖ Utilities to run the offices and plants [telephones, electricity, heat and air conditioning]
- ❖ Raw materials to produce their goods
- ❖ Postage to ship and distribute products to customers

❖ Promotional and marketing materials [brochures, catalogues, advertisements, and training manuals for the sales force]
❖ Taxes [State, local and federal]

Profits may be used to:

1. Build the business
2. Pay bonuses to employees
3. Pay dividends to stockholders.

1. **Building a business** can include:

❖ Creating more jobs
❖ Buying new or more equipment
❖ Distributing more promotional materials to attract additional customers, or
❖ Opening new divisions to cover more territory.

2. **Bonuses** may be paid to employees in the form of:

❖ Performance bonus – paid to employees whose actions and results help the business grow
❖ Holiday bonus – paid to all employees at the end of the year as appreciation for their service
❖ Profit or Gain-sharing bonuses – paid to a team or all employees when the company profits reach a certain level and/or they introduce a new product, concept, or process that generates a profit.

4. **Dividends** to stockholders – these are similar to interest on a savings account. When the company declares a profit, they often pass along part of this profit to Stockholders by

paying them a set amount of money for each share of stock they own. Stockholders sometimes have the option of receiving this dividend in the form of a check, or re-investing it into the company in exchange for additional shares of stock.

Businesses create annual budgets to determine how much money they will need each year. Budgets are the financial plan the company follows to generate profits by increasing sales and decreasing the expenses of running the business.

In the 1980s and 1990s, many companies reduced expenses to increase profits by cutting jobs. This process is called 'downsizing'. Downsizing also occurs after companies merge with or acquire other companies. When the resulting company has too many employees performing the same jobs, positions are eliminated to increase the business' efficiency.

You probably know someone who lost his or her job due to downsizing. When a company changes the way it does business, new and different jobs are often created, resulting in new opportunities for employees.

Non-Profit Businesses

Businesses that exist purely to provide services in their communities are called Non-Profit agencies, associations, foundations or organizations. They provide a service to their community to support social welfare, promote the arts, or advocate people's rights on a broad range of subjects.

'Non – profit' organizations generate income through fund-raising, donations, membership dues, or grants from the government or other 'Non-Profit' corporations.

The income covers operating expenses of providing the service. Excess income generated after operating expenses are paid is placed in a fund called 'Reserves'.
Reserves are used to run the organization in the following year, if needed to offer new services, or provide grants to other non-profits.

Non-profit organizations incur expenses similar to for-profit businesses [employees' compensation, office space, telephones, utilities, postage, and promotional materials] and establish a budget every year to determine how much they need to cover those expenses.

Some of the money collected is often distributed as grants to other non-profit businesses in a community. These may include homes for the elderly or infirm, shelters and soup kitchens for the homeless. Non-profit organizations may employ a small staff of paid employees or are run by volunteers.

Positions in non-profit organizations include Executive Director, Public Relations Manager, Business Development Director, and clerical staff. Volunteers, who do not get paid for the work they do, often help non-profit organizations. They do this for the gratification they receive from helping others.
In order to qualify for non-profit status, these organizations must have a Board of Directors and pass governmental guidelines.

Some non-profit organizations you may know include The United Way, Big Brothers and Big Sisters, American Red

Cross, Boy and Girl Scouts of America, and Police Athletic Leagues.

The United Way is a human service agency. It raises money to help other human service agencies. Money is raised through annual campaigns and charitable donations. Each year, United Way employees work with employees in 'for profit' businesses to set up campaigns to raise money for charitable causes.

Other non-profit organizations include public radio and television stations. They run annual fund – raising events during which they ask listeners or viewers to call in to pledge money for the station's programming. In exchange for your donation, you may receive a musical CD, tee shirt, video, mug or some other item bearing the station's name.

ORGANIZATIONAL STRUCTURE

A business may have one employee, a few, many or thousands. It may serve customers locally in small towns, statewide, regionally [several adjoining states], nationwide, or internationally. These factors influence the business' organizational structure.

The business' structure refers to the levels of employees and who reports to whom. The structure can be flat or have levels.

Flat structures apply to businesses that are run by one or a few employees. Employees in flat organizations share similar amounts of responsibility and often get an equal share of the rewards or profits. A small entrepreneurial consulting firm would be a flat organization. It usually consists of an owner, some consultants or associates and an administrative assistant.

A business with many employees and levels of responsibility is considered to have a *pyramid* structure. In these multi-level organizations, employees have different degrees of responsibility, and reap different degrees of reward and profits.

In each business, people assume various roles to assure that the business succeeds. The fewer the number of employees in a given business or organization, the more responsibility each one has for achieving the business or organization's strategic goals and objectives.

The more employees in a business or organization, the more specifically defined and narrow is each person's role and responsibilities.

Departments/functions

Businesses and organizations consist of various departments, each of which has a specific function within the business to meet strategic goals and objectives.
Each department and its employees are involved in some aspect of designing, manufacturing, selling, and delivering products and services to customers.

Typically, a manufacturing business that sells tangible products will have these functions:

- ❖ Customer Service
- ❖ Engineering
- ❖ Finance
- ❖ Human Resources

- ❖ Marketing (also called Public Relations)
- ❖ Manufacturing (also called Operations)
- ❖ Research & Development (may be part of Engineering)
- ❖ Quality Assurance
- ❖ Sales
- ❖ Shipping and Distribution (also called Warehousing) and
- ❖ General Administration.

A business that provides tangible and intangible services will normally have these functions:

- ❖ Customer Service
- ❖ Finance, Human Resources
- ❖ Marketing or Public Relations
- ❖ Operations
- ❖ Quality Control, and
- ❖ General Administration.

Both manufacturing and service businesses employ Information Systems [IS] and Legal departments or contract these services from independent providers. Within each department, functions may be further divided into organizational *Units*.

The employees in each unit perform work that contributes to the overall function of the department and ultimate success of the company.

Most businesses or organizations that sell products or services follow similar procedures to grow their business and serve customers. That procedure goes like this:

1. The Marketing department conducts research to determine what customers want/need and what competitors are selling.
2. The Engineering department develops prototypes of improved or new products or services that the business or organization will offer.
3. Marketing and Sales departments join together to test the new products or services with customers to find out how they like the new item or ask what improvements should be made.
4. The Manufacturing [or Operations] department designs the procedures and specifications [specs] to produce the new products and orders the raw materials for production.
5. The Finance department determines the price at which the products or services should be sold and how much the company needs to sell to meet their budget and generate a profit.
6. Sales staffs show products to customers and record *advance* orders to determine how many products are needed.
7. The Manufacturing or Operations department produces the products or services.
8. Customer Service and/or Sales representatives take orders from customers.
9. The Shipping and Distribution departments pack, label and ship the products to fill customer orders.

This procedure is repeated regularly to assure that a Company continues to serve its customers and retain its position in various markets.

Each department in the company performs its daily operations to address employees' and customers' needs.

a) <u>General Administration</u> monitors what's happening in the industry and the world in order to generate or modify plans that keep the Company profitable. They inform their staff of business objectives and observe how the company performs against plans.

b) <u>Human Resources</u> staff interviews candidates for vacant positions, administers benefits and payroll programs, conducts training programs, monitors performance and resolves disputes for existing employees.

c) <u>Customer Service</u> staff records telephone orders and answers customers' questions about their orders.

d) Employees in the <u>Finance department</u> check new customers' credit rating, record the money received for the sale of goods and services, pay bills and taxes.

e) Employees in <u>Information Systems</u> maintain business records and generate reports to tell management whether or not the business is running according to plans.

f) <u>Legal</u> staff may resolve employee relations disputes, investigate new business development deals, track the Company's compliance with government regulations, or investigate problems with competitors and international business issues.

Each major department consists of smaller business units. The units in Finance include Accounts Payable, Accounts Receivable, Billing, Credit, and Payroll. The Billing unit prepares the invoices/bills charging customers for the products or services they purchase and receive. Billing Unit employees also prepare statements telling customers how much money they owe the business every month. Accounts Payable is responsible for paying the invoices/bills the business receives from its suppliers or vendors. (Suppliers are other businesses that sell materials, products or services that a business needs to make its own products or provide its own services.)

Accounts Payable employees also pays bills necessary to maintain normal operations like rent, utilities and taxes and prepares and distributes employee paychecks.

Accounts Receivable records and deposits the money that customers send to the business for the products or services they purchased. The Credit unit analyzes customers' credit history to determine whether the Company should sell its products or services to them. Credit unit employees often recommend special arrangements for customers who have a poor credit history but still want to buy from the company.

The Human Resources department units include Benefits, Compensation, Employee Relations, Employment, and Training. The Benefits unit recommends which insurance, how much paid vacation and holidays employees should receive.

The Compensation staff determines the value of specific jobs and what employees will be paid for doing these jobs. It also assures that employees are paid properly.

Employee Relations personnel resolve employee disputes and make sure that the business complies with all government laws and guidelines for employees. Employment or Staffing employees interview candidates and recommend whom to hire for various jobs in the company. The Training unit staff develops and conducts training programs to ensure that employees have the skills to do the work they were hired to do.

A legal department is a group of attorneys/lawyers that the company hires as regular employees. They advise management about the laws on how to conduct business in their state, city/town, country, and internationally. They also work with Human Resources staff to resolve employee grievances in order to prevent lawsuits. If someone sues the company, the legal staff helps the company avoid or minimize liability and defends the company against the suit.

The Marketing Department units include Marketing Communications Market Research, and Product Management. Communications staff design packaging for the products, and develop materials that explain their products or services to customers and the sales staff.

Market Research staff asks customers for feedback about the company's products or services. Customers expect that their comments may result in the company offering new and/or improved products or services.

Product managers are the experts for a specific product and monitor the product's success. They work with other Marketing department staff to prepare advertising, track sales, and answer customers' questions about the product and assure that all materials are current.

Engineers design the company's products or services and establish the plans for manufacturing the products or delivering the service. The plans contain specifications [specs] for producing the product or services.

Specs are similar to blue prints or floor plans needed for building a house. The Manufacturing department uses the specs to produce the tangible products a business sells.

Engineers may be involved in training employees on how to deliver or explain the product(s) to customers.

In service companies, the specs are the processes or procedures that employees follow to provide services to the customers.

The Actuarial department in an Insurance company is the Engineering department. They design products like insurance policies and determine the criteria that customers must satisfy to buy the products.

The Research & Development (R&D) department scientists in a medically related company perform the engineering function.

The Sales function employees sell the company's products or services to customers. A sale occurs when a customer commits to buying what the company offers, and sends payment for the product or service delivered. Sales employees communicate with Engineering, R&D, Marketing, and Customer Service to assure that customers get what they purchase or order.

Most businesses have a Board of Directors, referred to simply as the Board. Board members are considered an advisory group.

Boards are at the top of the pyramid, and are responsible for approving budgets and expenditures for the business. This group makes decisions affecting the business's growth and profits.

LEVELS OF AUTHORITY

Employees in an organization are classified as executives, management or employees. Executives are the most senior level management employees in an organization.

Management positions are sometimes referred to as 'staff' positions. People who work in *management positions* are referred to as 'management'. They communicate the Board's objectives to their staff, and coordinate plans to achieve them.

Employees who report to management and occupy positions in the lower levels of the organization are referred to as 'line' employees', or associates. This term comes from the times when people worked in factories on assembly lines. Today, robots and machinery are programmed to perform some of the work that assembly line workers performed years ago.

Line employees titles include stock or billing clerks, customer service representatives, credit analysts, or telemarketers, and are often entry-level positions. They perform daily activities like stocking shelves, taking and filling customers' orders, paying bills, paying employees' salary, processing employee benefits claims, etc.

Management employees communicate business objectives to employees. Titles of the most senior executives include Chief Executive Officer (CEO), Chief Financial Officer (CFO), Chief Information Officer (CIO) and Chief Operating Officer (COO), Corporate Counsel (lawyers), and the President. The next level of executives is the Senior Vice Presidents.

Senior Vice Presidents report to the President. They manage specific business units (SBU) or divisions of the organization. For example, Pepsi Co. is the 'parent' company for many other well-known organizations. Pepsi Cola, Frito Lay, Taco Bell, Cadbury Schweppes, and Pizza Hut are all SBUs of Pepsi Co.

Senior Executives communicate the Board's objectives to the other managers in an organization, and inform the Board of Directors of the business' actual results against plans.

Senior Executives need the Boards' approval for many of the business decisions affecting strategies that they wish to implement. For example, if a company wants to give employees an annual bonus, the senior executives present their bonus plan to the Board of Directors.

The Board decides whether to issue the bonus, depending on how profitable the business was that year. The Board will also determine salary increases for the most senior executives.

The senior vice presidents' staff includes Vice Presidents and General Managers, the people responsible for overseeing the day-to-day operations of the business units or divisions.

The next levels of executives are the Directors, who report to the Vice Presidents and General Managers for each division. The Directors are responsible for managing a specific function within the division.

The next level of management is called middle management. Middle management positions include managers and supervisors who report to senior management.

These people carry out the Directors' instructions. Managers and supervisors monitor a staff of employees in the day-to-day activities of running the business. They observe their employees' work and evaluate the quality and quantity of their performance, or productivity.

Employees in Engineering, Marketing, Production, and Sales perform roles that directly produce or sell products or provide services to external customers. These roles include answering customers' questions, recording orders, or picking and packing items off warehouse shelves to fill the orders.
Employees in Finance and Human Resources perform roles that support a company's ability to serve its external customers by serving other employees, the internal customers.

Although still called line employees, you will find very few assembly lines in today's work place. Many companies have adopted the team concept. Teams are a group of people who work together and share different responsibilities. Team members are trained with an equal set of skills so they can fill in for each other depending on the situation. Teams are often organized in 'cells' or small stations within a factory or office environment. In manufacturing companies, entire products may be produced at a single station or cell.

The team decides who performs what tasks for the purpose of meeting or exceeding customers' expectations.

The Customer is always right!

CUSTOMERS

No business would succeed without customers. A customer is *anyone* who needs, uses, and/or buys the products or services that a company provides. Customers may be either external or internal.

External customers are people outside the business who buy products or services from a company. Employees in various departments are considered to be internal customers for each other.

These are your colleagues who may need you to complete a certain task or write a specific report in order for them to complete their job properly.

For example, the Human Resources department is a service function to all other departments. The Human Resources staff hires employees to perform jobs in other departments, conducts training programs to help employees in all departments do their jobs effectively, and assembles benefits packages for all employees. Similarly, employees in the Credit or Customer Service departments are customers for the Sales department. The Sales force often relies on employees in Credit or Customer Service to provide information for external customers. This information determines whether an external customer is financially sound – can pay their bills for products they wish to buy from the company.

Every employee is expected to serve the company's customers. In any job you hold, you will be both responsible for accomplishing certain tasks and activities, and accountable for making sure that you do your job properly.

RESPONSIBILITY AND ACCOUNTABILITY

Responsibilities are tasks and activities associated with your job that you are expected to perform. For example, a receptionist is responsible for answering the telephones, greeting visitors, and ordering office supplies.

Accountability is taking ownership of your responsibilities and admitting when you've done something well or poorly. When your team is accountable for its actions and responsibilities, you will receive praise for a job well done, or suggestions to improve poor results.

Every company and industry has its own set of standards and expectations regarding how things get done there.

CORPORATE CULTURE – 'RULES OF THE ROAD'

The Culture in a business organization means how things are done in that business. This includes values and beliefs that people share as well as what employees expect of each other. A company's culture is often evident in the office environment.

When you walk into any business, you can sense the business' 'personality' in the atmosphere. You can tell whether people enjoy working there and whether they are feeling stressed. You can tell this by the looks on their faces, the way they sit at their desks, and the way they walk around the office.

How do employees treat you and each other? Are they pleasant and cordial or distant and aloof? Do you see smiling faces and hear courteous exchanges between employees and telephone conversations, or do you see people frowning and being rude? These observations will give you a sense of the business' culture.

Most businesses have standards of conduct and rules, both written and unwritten, about how to behave. Often times, your level within the organizational structure dictates whom you talk to and what you must do to accomplish your objectives.

Executives and senior management have the most authority and responsibility and thus reap the highest rewards. Middle managers have more authority, responsibility, and bigger rewards than employees, though not as much as the senior executives.

Line employees have the least authority yet carry great responsibility and reap rewards for communicating with the customers and providing excellent customer service.

Regardless of where in an organization you start, there is always opportunity to rise to higher levels. Remember that *you can be and do anything you want as long as you have a plan and remain flexible* ☺

Learn what it takes to succeed in your particular company, and do the best job that you are capable of doing at all times. Know what you are responsible for. Take accountability for your actions, and continue to S O A R!

TIPS to S O A R [Seize Opportunities And Rewards]

❖ The purpose of business is to make money. A Company makes a <u>profit</u> when income exceeds expenses.

❖ Companies use various methods to generate income. Most often, they sell their goods or services to customers.

❖ Businesses use their income to pay their operating expenses and plan how much money they will need each year by creating annual budgets.

❖ The employees in each unit perform work that contributes to the overall function of the department and ultimate success of the company.

❖ Employees in an organization are classified as executives, management or employees.

❖ You are both responsible for accomplishing certain tasks and accountable for making sure that you do your job properly.

❖ *The Culture* in a business organization means how things are done in that business.

❖ All businesses need customers. A customer is *anyone* who needs, uses, and/or buys products or services that a company provides. Customers may be either external or internal.

❖ The customer is always right!

Which tips from chapter 2 do *you* value most?
List them here.

Everyone's a customer!

- CHAPTER 3 -

Well, Well, Well...
What do you know?

Let me think about that ...

If you had a business, what kind of employees would you hire?

WHAT EMPLOYERS WANT

Employers depend on employees to achieve the business objectives and help the company to succeed. In exchange for your salary, benefits, and opportunities that an employer gives you, you will be expected to perform your job well. Performing your job well means applying your knowledge, demonstrating the technical skills of your field, and getting along with people – customers, peers, colleagues, superiors, suppliers and vendors.

Employers look for employees who display a positive attitude, energy and enthusiasm for their work. Several skills are critical to succeeding in the workplace and life. All are important and used simultaneously.

Your job and employer may place higher priorities on some of these skills. In addition to reading, arithmetic calculations and computer savvy, employers will expect you to demonstrate sound business judgment, effective interpersonal skills. These include:

1. Communication (listening, speaking, and writing)
2. Thinking and reasoning
3. Problem solving and decision making
4. Planning and organizing
5. Results – orientation/Productivity
6. Flexibility
7. Team work, and
8. Leadership

Mastering each skill will help you use it effectively and appropriately in any situation. The more effectively you demonstrate these skills, the better will be your opportunities for growth and reward in your chosen profession.

Thinking is, by far, the foundation for all other skills. Many people find it difficult to think because it takes time and effort. Like all other skills, making thinking a habit requires practice.

THINKING AND REASONING

Clear thinking and reasoning are necessary to effectively identify and solve problems. In a business environment, you must train yourself to focus on what is good for the business.

Most of us believe that we are always thinking although it is not always apparent to others. Develop the habit of asking yourself questions in a given situation to demonstrate that you are thinking.

One example of the need to think in the workplace involves serving customers. You may be so eager to please a customer that you make promises before fully thinking whether you'll be able to deliver what you promise or how it will affect your company.

Before you promise a customer that they will receive a shipment overnight, be sure that this is possible. Think about all the other people involved with delivering what you promise.

Is the product is in stock? Can the shipping department pack and send the product in time to reach the customer overnight? Does the customer's credit history warrant this shipment and will he pay the additional charges for overnight delivery?

Also, when is the last pickup scheduled by the carrier service and will it reach the customer overnight?

Thinking about all aspects of your behavior and the business you work for may take some time, and will produce much better results than just operating on 'auto pilot'.

All learning requires you to think. You may not realize that there is a process for learning *how* to think. Your ability to think develops as you answer questions that you ask yourself or someone else asks you. Quite often, we answer automatically, without realizing that there were other answers we could have given.

Thinking means that you explore your options before giving an answer. This may happen very quickly, or take some time. For example, as you think about selecting or building your career, ask yourself the following questions:

1. What do I like to do that I would enjoy doing on a regular basis [What are my interests]?
2. Why do I like doing those things? [What is my motivation?]
3. What jobs are likely to provide opportunities for me to use those interests? [How can I find out what is available?]
4. How can I find jobs like these?
5. What is my plan to obtain such a job?
6. What is likely to happen if I follow my plan?
7. How will I feel if I accomplish my plan?
8. What will I do if I don't get the results that I expect from my plan?

In addition to the eight skills previously cited, several behavioral characteristics and habits that you can develop will increase your success in life as well as the workplace.

These include accountability, adaptability, integrity (honesty), reliability, and dependability [the commitment to do what you say you will and complete what you start].

Work is just that - WORK. It takes focused effort and concentration on completing specific tasks to achieve the objectives and goals you set. You can still enjoy your work and have fun in the process. Just stay focused on what you're expected to do and agreed to when you accepted your position.

I never did a day's work in my life. It was all fun. - Thomas A. Edison

In order to know which skill(s) to use when, observe your organization - the culture, the nature of the business, who the key players are, and the key issues or challenges facing your company. Jumping in too quickly may cause embarrassment if you haven't learned the best way to communicate your ideas in your environment.

I was often embarrassed in my earlier career. Due to my energy and enthusiasm, I had a tendency to speak up, and often finished other people's statements for them, cutting them off mid-sentence. When I did this at staff meetings, I was embarrassed because my colleagues and boss looked at me like I was from another planet.
I've learned to wait for people to finish their thoughts before offering mine. My mind still races ahead of the conversation on hand, but now, I silently monitor what goes on in my mind before saying it. When I've thought through what I want to say and am sure that it's my turn to speak, I offer my suggestion or opinion as appropriate.

As a result, my co-workers listen to me and give me the courtesy of considering my ideas more fully.

You've seen that a business' purpose is to make money. Good business decisions are based on whether the outcome is good for the business, will help it achieve its objectives, or whether it is likely to be bad for or hurt the business. Poor business decisions either use resources (money, people, equipment, and time) poorly or cost more than the expense will gain in return.

Senior and middle managers are paid large salaries to make decisions that will help and are good for the business. Line employees are also expected to make wise business decisions.

The sooner you learn to make rational, logical, wise decisions about the business, the better you will be viewed by others, particularly senior management. The better management thinks of you, the more you will be considered when promotional opportunities are available.

When you offer a suggestion to your supervisor about something you would like to do, he or she may accept or reject it on the basis of its merit to the business, not on whether they like you and think it's a good idea. When you learn not to take others' decisions personally, and look at how they impact the business, you will increase your chances of growing with the business and earning more recognition and reward.

When you identify a problem in your organization, write it down on a piece of paper. Seeing it in writing often helps you recognize various aspects of the problem to generate possible solutions. Any time that you inform your boss about a problem you've identified, it's important that you tell him or her specifically what the problem is, why it's a problem, and what you suggest be done to correct it. Supervisors, especially senior management, respect employees who are able to recognize situations that may be harmful to the business, and can suggest viable solutions to fix the problem.

If you bring only problems to your boss without any solutions, you will be viewed as a whiner, a complainer, and a troublemaker. These types of employees develop unfavorable reputations.

INTERPERSONAL RELATIONS

"To disregard what the world thinks of us is not only arrogant but utterly shameless." - Cicero

No one works completely alone. Regardless of how much you enjoy your privacy, when you work for an organization [even your own firm] you must deal with others to accomplish your work and achieve your objectives.

Succeeding in the workplace and life means learning how to treat others with respect and dignity [even if you don't like them] and making a sincere effort to cooperate with and be considerate of others' needs. Developing good interpersonal relationships with others depends first on knowing, accepting and approving of yourself. Then you can easily work effectively with others and build successful relationships in the workplace and life.

Sometimes, despite your good intentions, you will say or do things that others interpret as inappropriate or ineffective. When this happens, you may be embarrassed and scold yourself for your actions.

Human nature tends to make you harder on yourself than others would be on you. You'll fear that others are thinking equally badly of you as you do yourself.

Fear exaggerates a situation and you expect the worst. If you make a mistake, acknowledge and apologize for it. You'll find that people will forgive interpersonal blunders as long as you accept your part in it and don't repeat the same ones routinely.

Get over it! In a few weeks, days, or even hours, your incident will most likely be forgotten. Effective workers know that it's 'back to business as usual' if the business is to succeed. Staying focused on your critical priorities and effective performance will help to diffuse the pain from prior errors or ineffectiveness.

PLANNING & ORGANIZATION SKILLS

You've probably heard the cliché, "If you don't know where you're going, every road will take you there." This means if you don't have a plan, you won't achieve the outcome you desire.

Author Lewis Carroll explained this concept in "Alice in Wonderland" this way: "Would you please tell me which way I ought to go from here?" asked Alice. "That depends a good deal on where you want to get," said the cat. "I'm not really too sure of my destination," replied Alice. "Then it doesn't matter which way you go," said the cat.

These skills will be covered in depth in the following chapters. Once you've developed competence in them, always be aware of ways to continue to grow and learn how to apply them in different situations.

You probably think that once you're through with school, you don't need to study any more. On the contrary, the business world requires employees at all levels to learn continuously. Learning improves your skills, which will increase your value to your organization.

In the audiocassette program, "Embracing Chaos", Tom Peters tells a story from his high school years about visiting a friend's home. After dinner, his friend's father, a surgeon, went to his den to study procedures that he would use for the next day's operations. Tom realized then that studying never stops. Even when you've finished your formal education, it is necessary to refresh your mind about the techniques and skills necessary to do a certain part of your job.

Businesses recognize and value employees who understand the importance of continuous learning throughout life. The knowledge and expertise that you develop will open new doors and present new opportunities to you throughout your career.

Behavioral scientists explain the human learning cycle as follows:

Stage 1. **Unconsciously incompetent** - Unaware of what you don't know.
Stage 2. **Consciously incompetent** - Knowing what you don't know.
Stage 3. **Consciously competent** - Knowing what you're supposed to do and practicing it repeatedly.
Stage 4. **Unconsciously competent** - Consistently applying learned skills effectively in new situations.

Stage 1 says that we have a blind spot to skills that we have yet to learn. When we recognize or receive feedback from someone else that we need to develop a specific skill, we become aware of the things that we don't know. This moves us from stage one to two.

With focused determination, we gather information that we need to learn a new skill and then practice it until we get it right. This moves us from stage two to stage three of the learning cycle.

By repeatedly applying newly found knowledge, we develop and use the new skills without having to think about them. This takes us to the fourth stage of the learning cycle.

The next chapters will explore the skills covered here in depth.

TIPS TO S O A R [Seize Opportunities And Rewards]

❖ Employers need and depend on employees to achieve the business objectives and help the company to succeed.

❖ In exchange for salary, benefits, and growth opportunities, an employer expects you to perform your job well.

❖ In addition to reading, arithmetic calculations and computer savvy, employers expect you to demonstrate sound business judgment and effective interpersonal skills.

❖ The more effectively you demonstrate these skills, the better will be your opportunities for growth and reward in your chosen profession.

❖ *Thinking* is, by far, the foundation for all other skills. Like all the other skills, thinking requires practice.

❖ The habits of accountability, adaptability, integrity (honesty), reliability, dependability and treating others with respect and dignity help you succeed in the workplace and life.

❖ You must deal with others to accomplish your work and achieve your objectives.

❖ Businesses recognize and value employees who understand the importance of continuous learning throughout life.

What tips from chapter 3 do *you* value most?
List them below:

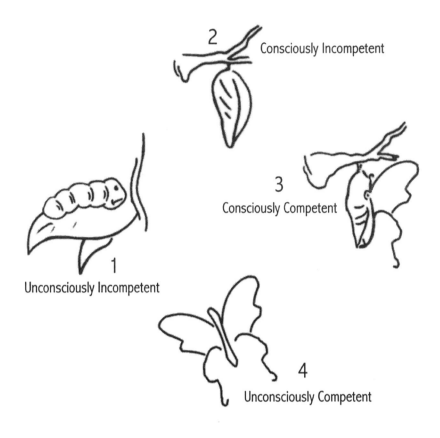

2 Consciously Incompetent

3 Consciously Competent

1 Unconsciously Incompetent

4 Unconsciously Competent

The learning cycle ... A process of transformation.
Grow your dreams, spread your wings, and S O A R!

- CHAPTER 4 -

You think *You've* got problems?

Yeah, that's the ticket...

You want WHAT? NO PROBLEM...

*"Before it can be solved, a problem must be clearly stated
and defined" - William Feather*

Life is about choices! The workplace and life will give you
many opportunities to make choices. Many people approach
every choice or decision as a problem that needs to be solved.

Some choices will be clear-cut. You'll know immediately which
option you want, like what to eat for lunch. Some choices will
appear as simple *dilemmas* that need to be settled, such as
which movie to see, or where to go on vacation. Still others will
appear as *problems* that need to be solved like when your
computer or car suddenly stops working and you don't know
why.

Some people say they have a problem when what they face is
simply a dilemma or uncertainty. A true *problem* exists when
your results are different than what you expect and you don't
know why. View each 'problem' as a 'challenge' to be met. This
will make it seem like a puzzle or game instead of a burden.

Solving problems involves gathering information, generating
solutions and choosing the best decision. Resolving a dilemma
or uncertainty also involves making choices.

Problem solving starts with recognizing that a problem exists.
For example, suppose your computer suddenly stops after it
worked perfectly for weeks. If you don't know why it stopped,
you have a *problem*. You expected it to continue working
properly and are not sure why it stopped.

If someone asks you what you would like to do for the weekend or what you want for lunch, and you don't have a definite answer, you are *uncertain*. When you have difficulty choosing what movie to see from among three that you would like to see equally as much as the others, you have a *dilemma*. A dilemma is when you have to choose between alternatives of equal value.

Resolving problems requires gathering information, thinking critically about that information, and then deciding what to do about it. Once you analyze your facts, generate the options available to you and choose the best one. Choosing the best one means making a decision. Solving problems requires you to think!

Resolving dilemmas and uncertainties simply means declaring your choice from the options available to you. In some cases, you may want additional information, but uncertainties and dilemmas do not require the same degree of gathering and analyzing information that solving problems does.

The best way to start gathering information is by asking open-ended questions. You'll remember these from English class as those questions that begin with Who, What, When, Where, Why, and How?

To resolve a problem, follow this simple process, thinking critically at each step to achieve a desirable outcome.

1. Identify the specific problem in exact terms.
2. List all possible causes for the problem.
3. Think of potential solutions for each cause.
4. Determine the likely consequences of applying each solution.

[Generate a list of potential issues or additional problems that implementing each solution might cause].

5. Determine how you would address each of *those* potential issues.
6. Select and apply the best* solution to the problem.
7. Monitor results.
8. Evaluate the actual results against desired results.

*   The best possible solution is the one that solves the *original* problem without generating additional problems.

When the problem is fixed to everyone's satisfaction, you have found a good solution. If the problem remains, repeat steps 4 – 8 until you select the best solution and the problem is resolved.

First you must determine that a problem exists. Remember that a problem exists when the results you achieve are different than the results that you expected. Let's look at an example of a problem in a business that manufactures books.

A customer calls the Customer Service department to report that he did not receive all the items that he ordered and the ones he did receive were damaged.

This is a 'problem' because the results are not what you or the customer expected to happen and you don't know why it happened. Both of you expected that he would receive exactly the items that he ordered, undamaged, and on time.

Step 1: *Identify the specific problem.* – Mr. Smith ordered fifteen cases of books worth $22,425 and only received nine cases. Three of the cases he received were crushed, rendering the books useless.

Step 2: *Think of possible causes for the problem* – ask questions to find out which, if any of these causes is the reason for the problem. Be sure to get answers to questions that begin with Who, What, When, Where, Why, and How? To activate your thinking process, the first question to ask is, *What could make this happen?*

Then ask a series of other questions to generate possible causes. [You might ask an employee from the carrier service to be part of the problem-solving team]

❖ **Who** took Mr. Smith's order, **who** communicated the order to Shipping and **who** picked, packed, and shipped the order?

❖ **What** conditions did we agree to when shipping the order to Mr. Smith? **What** would Mr. Smith like us to do to correct this problem?

❖ **When** was the order picked, packed and shipped? **When** did the carrier service pick it up, and **when** did we agree that Mr. Smith would receive it?

❖ **Where** did we send the order?

❖ **How** was Mr. Smith's order processed and how many cartons did the original order say Mr. Smith requested?

❖ **How** was the order transported to Mr. Smith? Which carrier did we use?

❖ **Why** did any deviations from the plan occur?

In asking these questions you may discover the following facts:
❖ The person who took Mr. Smith's order may not have understood him.
❖ The person who took Mr. Smith's order may be incapable of properly entering the order into the computer.

❖ The person who took Mr. Smith's order may lack the knowledge to properly record and execute the order, or may have made a mistake.
❖ The computer or order entry software program may not be working correctly.
❖ The person who picked, packed, and shipped the order may not have read the order slip or the book titles accurately when he or she picked the items off of the shelf.
❖ The delivery person may have delivered the wrong packages to Mr. Smith.
❖ The delivery service may not have delivered all the books to Mr. Smith.
❖ Mr. Smith may have told you the wrong product codes and number of books that he wanted.

What other questions will you ask to find out if any of these caused the problem?

Sometimes, just asking the right questions will generate the exact source of the problem and you can easily fix it.

If, after answering all of the questions, you don't know why Mr. Smith only received some of his order, you now have an unhappy customer. Proceed to step 3.

Step 3: *Think of possible _solutions_ to each cause.* You could:
❖ Ask Mr. Smith to check the mailing label to assure that he got the right packages.
❖ Ask Mr. Smith to repeat the product codes and exact titles of the books that he ordered.
❖ Call the delivery service to assure they did their part correctly; if not, have them correct the problem immediately.

❖ Send Mr. Smith the additional six cases through the same carrier and replace the three damaged cases at no charge.

❖ Use a different carrier service to deliver the additional cases and replace the damaged ones.

❖ Arrange to personally deliver the additional cases and replacements to Mr. Smith.

❖ Ask Mr. Smith to come to your office to pick up the additional cases and replacements.

❖ Make sure that the person entering the order is properly trained, has good vision, hearing and keyboarding skills, and can operate a computer.

❖ Make sure that the computer and order-entry program are working properly. Train the employee and fix the computer program if necessary.

Step 4: *Determine the likely consequences of applying each solution.*

❖ Sending Mr. Smith additional and replacement cases *may* result in the same or similar problems.

❖ The employees who process the order *may* have difficulty performing their tasks accurately, in which case you have some human resources issues to address.

❖ Unless the problem is rectified to Mr. Smith's satisfaction, you *could* lose his business, which could affect the company's income. [An order of this size is not likely to have that great an impact on the business, but if this problem is repeated with other customers, it could affect the annual budget.]

Step 5: Determine how you would address each of these issues:

❖ Someone would have to deliver the products directly to assure their safe arrival.

❖ Employees may need to be re-trained or replaced with more competent ones.

❖ The sales team will need to generate additional orders.

Steps 6 - 8: Apply the best solution, monitor results, and evaluate them against the desired outcome.

For argument's sake, let's say you discovered that the error was with the carrier. You switch to a new carrier, and Mr. Smith's order was sent and received as expected. Problem solved!

If the problem were not corrected, you would need to think about why not, and repeat the problem – solving process until you pick and apply the best solution. If all of your initial ideas do not generate a solution, think of other options that you can apply or ask other employees for their input. Sometimes a fresh perspective generates better ideas. Keep repeating this process until you have found the correct solution.

Very often, people see a problem and act upon the first solution that pops into their mind. This solution may work, or it may create other problems. *Thinking* about the problem will help you generate a list of many possible solutions. Even if the first solution you think of is a good one, it's always wise to ask, what other options are there?

Further thinking helps you determine the potential outcome of each solution and narrows down your choices to the best one.

Picking the best solution will save you time and money without creating other problems. When you identify problems and suggest effective solutions, you will earn a reputation for being a thoughtful and valuable employee.

To resolve a dilemma or uncertainty, simply identify the options that you have. Quickly determine which option will give you the best results and select it. Delaying a decision for too long could tire you and result in lost opportunities.

When you're uncertain about making a choice, talk to people who have faced similar situations. Ask them what made them select what they did and how satisfied they were with their results.

COURAGE TO CHOOSE

When you are asked to choose something and answer "I don't care", you allow other people to choose for you. When you let others make your decisions for you, you forfeit the right to complain if you don't like the results. Refusing to choose an option or decide that one is better than another is to declare yourself powerless. You may also damage relationships with people who get tired of having the responsibility of making decisions for you.

Solving problems and dilemmas is simply a matter of gathering facts about the situation, looking at your options and then choosing one to see if it solves the problem or dilemma.

When you face a problem or dilemma, stop to recognize what choices you have, and then select one. Choosing an option means that you've decided it is the best for the situation right now. It may not necessarily be the option that you always choose, but it's better to make a choice than to put it off indefinitely. Of course, one option you have is to not decide right now. By not deciding, you've made a decision not to act on the situation.

Once you've made your decision, act on it – implement it! If it turns out that you've selected the wrong solution to a problem, simply go back to the other options you didn't choose, and see if one of them solves the problem. Keep trying solutions until you find the one that solves the problem.

Continually refusing to make choices or decisions will erode your self-esteem and self-confidence and cause other people to doubt your ability. This may mean that you miss out on some great opportunities, learning experiences and a lot of fun.

Remember when your mother asked you to taste a new food? You may have turned up your nose, stuck out your tongue and made a face at the thought of it without even knowing what it tasted like. If your mother forced you to try it, you often found out that you really liked it. Imagine what you would miss if you refused to ever taste pizza, hamburgers, french fries or ice cream!

Every time you exert your freedom to choose and voice your opinion, you take control of your own destiny. When someone asks you to state your decision or choice, tell yourself, "I CAN do this!" and then declare your choice or decision.

Making choices is like looking for the right piece in a jigsaw puzzle. Pick up one piece to see if it fits the open space. If it doesn't, put it down and try another piece. By process of elimination you know which pieces don't fit that particular space. Continuing to try different pieces helps you complete the whole puzzle. Then you have a beautiful picture in front of you as a reminder of your hard work and willingness to try different pieces.

When faced with a number of options or choices, try one to see if it 'fits' the situation. If it does, you're more confident and willing to make another choice. If it doesn't, you've whittled down the choices that you have left. Through process of elimination, you will find the choice that you like the best and will develop the skill of making choices.

In the workplace, you will face many situations where you need to declare your choice and voice your opinion. Do so with confidence.

Starting with your job interview, you will be asked what kind of work you like to do. Depending on how much experience you have, you may not yet know exactly what kind of work you would like to do. You'll still need to give the interviewer enough information about you to show them that you're *willing* to make a choice, once you understand what your options are.

COMMUNICATING PROBLEMS

Think carefully about *how* you are going to communicate a 'problem' and your suggested remedy. Sometimes it is best to speak to your supervisor privately about an issue before bringing it to others' attention. If your supervisor is difficult to reach, leave a note for him or her indicating what the issue is and asking for a time when you can discuss it in detail.

We often hear that 'two heads are better than one'. Ask others for their ideas when solving a problem. It will give you a broad perspective of the potential causes and help you to generate and select the best solution.

Be sure to think before you speak. Others will pay more attention to you and take your suggestions seriously if they know that you've thought about them before blurting them out. If you habitually act impulsively, learn to slow down. Take a deep breath, and ask yourself, "What would be the best way for me to approach this situation? What should I say or do?" Thinking through the best way to approach a situation will save you a good deal of embarrassment and will increase the likelihood of you getting the results you want.

When you observe a situation that you believe is a problem, offer a solution. If you believe something is a problem and you are not willing to offer a solution, then don't continuously complain about it. Others will view your continuous complaining as whining, and you will develop a reputation for having a poor attitude and being an ineffective communicator.

Effective problem solving often requires taking the initiative and asserting yourself to identify problems that are opportunities for improving your company. We'll discuss Initiative and Assertiveness skills will in the next chapter.

TIPS TO S O A R [Seize Opportunities And Rewards]

❖ Life is about choices! Many people approach every choice or decision as a problem that needs to be solved. Some are simply a dilemma or uncertainty.

❖ A true *problem* exists when your results are different than what you expect and you don't know why.

❖ Solving problems involves gathering information, generating solutions, and choosing the best decision.

❖ The best possible solution is the one that solves the original problem without generating additional problems.

❖ The best way to start gathering information is by asking open-ended questions that begin with Who, What, When, Where, Why, and How?

❖ Once you've made your decision, act on it – implement it! If you've selected the wrong solution, select another options until you find the one that solves the problem.

❖ Refusing to choose an option or decide that one is better than another is to declare yourself powerless. Continually refusing to make choices or decisions will erode your self-esteem and self-confidence.

❖ Think carefully about *how* you are going to communicate a 'problem' and your suggested remedy.

Which tips from chapter 4 do *you* value most?
List them here:

This will fix that problem ...

- CHAPTER 5 -

Whose life is this anyway?

Who influences *your* attitude and performance?

"There is no man living that can not do more than he thinks he can." - Henry Ford

Your thoughts determine your actions, and your actions determine your results. **Whether you think you can, or you think you can't, you're right.** The results you produce are translated into productivity.

The effort and skills that you exert to perform your job will determine the results you achieve. The effort that you exert to achieve your personal goals will result in the knowledge and self-confidence that *you can be, do and have anything you set your mind to.*

Your productivity is part of the value that you bring to an organization. The more and better the quality results that you produce, the higher your productivity [output] rating and the ultimate value that you bring to your customers, colleagues, and company. You will be held accountable for the results that you produce.

ACCOUNTABILITY

Accountability means accepting responsibility and ownership for your thoughts and actions even if things don't turn out as you expect. It means saying what you'll do, doing what you say you will, and admitting that you were responsible for the resulting outcomes – positive or negative.

When you accept accountability for your decisions and actions, you earn respect and a reputation for being honest, dependable, and trustworthy.

RESULTS-ORIENTATION

Results-orientation starts as an attitude that you are *willing* to do whatever it takes to achieve desired outcomes or results. Your attitude translates into actual results through your thoughts, words and actions. When you focus on achieving the desired results, your mind will discover the best means of achieving them. You demonstrate a results – oriented attitude when you:

- Show up for work, meetings, and scheduled appointments on time.
- Perform the work assigned to you, willingly and competently.
- Plan your work, and work your plan.
- Look for opportunities to participate in projects that will achieve the company's strategic plan and objectives.
- Use time effectively and efficiently, especially 'surprise' time. [This is time that you had scheduled, but is freed up at the last minute due to cancellations, others' scheduling conflicts, delays in receiving materials, etc.]
- Devote your time at work to **work** rather than personal issues or goofing off.
- Focus on relevant activities that help you accomplish the desired results rather than shuffling papers, walking around aimlessly or wasting time just to *look* busy.

There are many good reasons to achieve the results that you agree to perform or were hired to produce.

You will demonstrate to your employer that he or she made a wise decision and investment by hiring you. This builds others' confidence in you and is likely to extend your continued employment while exposing you to additional opportunities within your company.

You will acquire new knowledge and skills, which will earn you additional respect and opportunities in the larger workplace.

Your supervisor may recognize and reward your consistent results with a merit increase.

If you want to be viewed as a leader and assume leadership roles at work or in your community, results-orientation will increase others' perceptions of you as being a leader.

Perhaps the most important outcome of your results-orientation is the pride and sense of accomplishment that you reap from doing a good job. The more results-oriented you are, the more competent you will become at taking care of yourself.

Each time that you achieve the results that you set out to, you will gain the courage to produce results in all areas of your life. This will increase your ability to make decisions. An ability to make decisions will help you get more of what you want in life.

When you are part of a team, your results-orientation will inspire others to follow suit. Work and life become easier and more pleasant when everyone does their part to achieve desired results. People enjoy being around individuals who get things done and make things happen.

Many situations in work and life will require you to quickly assess a situation and act accordingly. This is results-orientation – focusing your efforts on obtaining the results that you and others want and need and then acting to make them happen.

While we all wish to earn respect from others, developing *self*-respect, confidence and esteem is most critical to succeeding in the workplace and life. Whether or not you receive tangible rewards from others, the intangible rewards that you give yourself will carry you throughout your life and generate rewards far greater than money can ever buy.

No one can ever take away your pride of accomplishment. The following poem illustrates the importance of positive self-worth, fueled through results-orientation and doing a good job:

Man in the Glass by Dale Winbrough

When you get what you want in your struggle for self
And the world makes you king for a day,
Just go to a mirror and look at yourself,
And see what *that* man has to say.

For it isn't your mother or father or spouse,
Whose judgement upon you must pass,
The fellow whose verdict counts most in your life,
Is the man staring back from the glass.

Some people may think you're a straight-shooting chum,
And call you a wonderful guy,
But the man in the glass says you're only a bum,
If you can't look him straight in the eye.

He's the fellow to please,
Never mind all the rest,
For he's with you clear up to the end,
And you've passed your most dangerous, difficult test,
If the man in the glass is your friend.

You may fool the whole world
Down your pathway of life
And get pats on your back as you pass,
But your final reward will be heartache and tears,
If you've cheated the man in the glass.
What other benefits can you think of for being results-oriented?

Word spreads quickly throughout a company and industry about the people who produce good results. Unfortunately, word spreads just as fast about employees who don't do good work, appear to be lazy and are unwilling to devote the effort to serve customers and help the company succeed. Being productive increases your success in the workplace and life.

PRODUCTIVITY

Your ***productivity*** refers to how much work you do and results that *you* achieve, or produce.

This is how *much* work you perform - i.e., how many projects you complete or products you produce within a specific timeframe. Your employer determines your productivity by *measuring* your results.

There are many ways to measure your results. Each industry and employer sets its own standards to measure an employee's productivity and performance. Employers set different standards and measurements for each job that their employees perform.

For example, if you are a member of a manufacturing team that produces computer parts, your supervisor will measure how many parts your team produces by the hour, day, week, month, quarter, or year. This standard measurement may be different at Gateway than it is at Dell Computers.

If you are in the sales department, your supervisor may measure or count the number of calls that you make. He or she will measure how many customers you spoke to, how many sales you made and the total sales dollars that you generated daily, weekly, monthly, quarterly, or annually.

If you choose to work as a social worker in a human *service* agency, the number of clients or cases that you see in the course of a week, month, or quarter will determine your productivity.

In education, the number of students taught and the number who graduate to the next grade may measure a teacher's performance.

In the food industry, management evaluates the wait staff's performance by measuring the number of customers served and customers satisfied.

We saw in chapter 2 that businesses exist to make money. A business generates money by selling products or services to customers. Every employee in a company is involved in some aspect of serving customers.

MORE ABOUT CUSTOMERS

Customers are the people who buy a company's *products*. Retail stores and manufacturers that build and provide tangible products have customers. For example, think of the stores where you buy clothes, food, instruments or sporting equipment. You are that store's customer. Likewise, the place where you buy those items had to buy the products from the manufacturer or a distributor. The storeowner is the manufacturer's customer.

The people who buy a company's *services* are often called **clients**. Lawyers, financial analysts and consultants have clients. If you need an attorney's help, you will be his or her client because he or she is providing a service to you rather than delivering a consumable product. Or, if you decide to hire a tutor to help you study for an important test, you are the tutor's *client* because the tutor is providing a service to you. People who work in the medical profession serve **patients**. Those who work in the field of education serve **students**.

Whatever they're called, the people you serve will be your business' *customers*. They will use or purchase whatever you are offering or selling and will have definite opinions about your performance. Every employee in an organization has some role in serving its customers.

Anyone within or outside your company who relies on the work that you do to help them is a customer.

Your supervisor will most likely take customers' comments into account when evaluating your performance, and productivity.

Your desire to do a good job will determine your results and level of productivity. When you truly want to do a good job, you will devote time and effort to acquiring the knowledge and information, and developing the skills necessary to do what you are expected to.

The following will help you perform to the best of your abilities and be considered as productive and results-oriented:

- a 'can-do attitude'
- a clear understanding of your role
- attention to specific goals and objectives that you're expected to achieve, perform or produce
- knowledge of the company's standard operating procedures [SOPs] that govern how you accomplish your results
- the resources [people, equipment, time, and money] necessary to produce the expected results, and
- honest feedback from a respected person or people on how well you are progressing.

Your attitude is, by far, the most important factor in determining your productivity. Developing a 'can-do' attitude and honest desire to perform will fuel your efforts to serve your customers and perform your job. When you focus on your productivity [achieving results], you will think more clearly and accomplish your goals despite whatever challenges or obstacles you may encounter.

When you consistently perform your job and focus on the end results, your visibility in an organization and job satisfaction will increase as well as your productivity. Develop a reputation for working hard versus hardly working.

Identify conditions that could be improved and suggest methods for improvement to your supervisor. Being results-oriented and productive means observing situations and taking the initiative to create procedures and practices that help the company to succeed.

INITIATIVE

Taking the initiative means being the first to introduce a new idea, try a new concept, or explore a good opportunity. Rather than wait for someone to tell you what to do, identify the things you can do to improve your productivity.

Instead of complaining about conditions that you don't like, think of how to improve them and suggest improved methods or techniques to your supervisor. Be careful, however, not to act too quickly in situations. If your actions appear rash, and are not well thought out, you could create problems that may be difficult to resolve.

For example, suppose you've learned that a new division is being formed in the company.

You think that there might be some interesting positions in that new division that could mean a promotion for you. You are so confident that you could contribute well in a new role, that you call the Vice President of the new organization to tell him how interested you are in working for him.

He might be impressed with your initiative and enthusiasm, and agree to talk to you about a potential position. Before the two of you reach an agreement, your boss and the Vice President in your current organization find out that you've gone directly to the management in the other division without first consulting them. They could be angry that you asserted yourself without going through the proper channels and accuse you of going around them for your own benefit. This is not viewed as having the best interest of your current division in mind and could damage your reputation throughout the entire company.

Each one of us wants to be recognized for doing a good job. How we want to be recognized for doing a good job is a personal matter. We'll explore this in Chapter 10 on behavioral styles.

ACCOUNTABILITY

Once you're committed to doing a good job, know exactly what's expected of you in your role. You can begin to learn about this during the interview process. Ask for a copy of the job description that outlines the tasks that the employee in that job would be expected to perform.

Ask each person that you speak with what he or she believes you will be expected to do on your job, and what type of work he or she is likely to need your help on. You will find that each employee you meet has his or her own idea of what the person performing the role you're interviewing for should do. Listen to these different opinions to learn about the company and understand different expectations.

The person whom you eventually report to is the person whose expectations are most critical. He or she will know what the company's business objectives are, and will help you understand what role you play in achieving these objectives. He or she will also evaluate your performance as to how well you meet the performance expectations that you agreed to.

Develop a results-oriented attitude and maintain your productivity. Focus on doing your job well and achieving results rather than getting caught up in company gossip or whining that conditions aren't what you'd like them to be.

Once you are hired for a position, discuss your performance expectations with your supervisor. These include the tasks that you are responsible for performing, and the results that you are expected to achieve. When you accept a job you accept responsibility to perform the expected tasks and agree to be held accountable for your results.

Your supervisor will give you feedback about how well you are managing your responsibilities and accountabilities. Once a year, this will be one topic of your *Performance Appraisal.*

This process is used to evaluate and reward each employee's performance every year just like report cards were used to evaluate your performance in school.

Your supervisor will monitor your performance throughout the year, informally, and once a year, formally during your Performance Appraisal Review.

This process assures that employees are doing the work they were hired to do, in the manner that they're expected to do it.

Companies use specific criteria to determine how well an employee performed his or her job. The criteria measure your actual results, [the quantity you produced or performed] and the skills and traits [the quality of your work] that you demonstrated while performing your work.

Some of the criteria are results-orientation, productivity, initiative and teamwork. Other factors that contribute to the quality of your work and how you performed it include your attendance, communication, time management, problem-solving and decision-making skills.

In many companies, your performance appraisal rating will determine whether or not you receive a raise in salary and how much of an increase you will get. Raises awarded for results you achieve are called *merit* increases. Companies that are unionized, pay a Cost Of Living Adjustment [COLA] to union employees. This raise is part of the union agreement and is not tied to an employee's results in the same way that merit raises are.

When companies establish their annual budgets, they allocate money for their employees' merit increases based on the company's profitability for that year.

Every employee in any organization has a role in achieving the company's strategic business objectives. Some employees are natural go-getters, constantly looking for better ways to do their job and improve the business. Others are content to just get by and believe that they are entitled to their paycheck just for showing up in the morning.

Which type of employee will you be?

TIPS TO S O A R [Seize Opportunities And Rewards]

❖ Your thoughts determine your actions, and your actions determine your results. Whether you think you can, or you think you can't, you're right.

❖ The more and better quality results that you produce, the higher your productivity [output] rating and the ultimate value that you bring to your customers, colleagues, and company.

❖ Results-orientation starts as an attitude that you are *willing* to do whatever it takes to achieve the desired outcome or results.

❖ There are many good reasons to achieve the results that you agree to perform, most importantly your sense of pride and belief in your own abilities.

❖ Your attitude is, by far, the most important factor in determining your productivity.

❖ Every employee in a company is involved in producing the company's products or providing the services to customers.

❖ Instead of complaining about conditions that you don't like, suggest improved methods or techniques to your supervisor.

❖ When you accept a job you accept responsibility to perform the expected tasks and will be held accountable for your results.

❖ Your performance is measured against what you're expected to do.

Which tips from chapter 5 do *you* value most?
List them here:

"Per my observations, Jodi, your
performance last year met or exceeded..."

- CHAPTER 6-

You want it *WHEN?*

There's no time like the present ... Do it NOW!

"You will never find time for anything. If you want time, you must make it."
   Charles Bixton

Time is one of our most precious resources. We get it for free and have the right to decide what we will do with it. How often do you or others complain about not having enough time? You know that we all have the same 24 hours or 1440 minutes a day, seven days a week, 52 weeks a year! No matter how clever, talented or creative you are or which calendar you use, you cannot create more time than this. What you *can* do is choose how to spend your time and what you'll do or accomplish with it.

In order to choose how to best use your time, you need to know what you want to accomplish with it.

Once you know **what** you want to have or accomplish [results], create a plan on **how** to get it [process]. When your plan is written, focus on carrying it out. The best way to create a rewarding career and fulfilling life is to plan your work, and work your plan.

Decide where you want to go, or what you want to achieve in life by establishing *goals*.

Goals are the specific results or outcomes that you want to achieve or the destination that you want to reach. Goals are WHAT you seek to create or accomplish.

Objectives are the specific tasks and activities that you perform to achieve your goals. Objectives are part of your plans.

Plans are the written documents that explain HOW you will achieve your goals and objectives. They are like roadmaps that help you navigate your journey to the destinations that you want to reach. They're like blueprints that you need to build a house, or the recipe that you follow to prepare a certain dish.

Planning is the process of establishing your goals, objectives and written plans. In planning, you define exactly *how* you will achieve your desired results, what resources you will need to do so, and the timeframe in which you will accomplish each task or activity.

Organization is arranging your plans in an orderly or sequential manner and working systematically to assure that you accomplish what you set out to do.

Successful people write their goals to make them tangible and concrete. An unwritten goal is simply a wish or hope. Writing your goals on a concrete surface lets you look at them daily. Writing goals makes it easier to draft a plan to achieve them.

People who write their goals accomplish them more than people who carry their goals around in their head. When you keep your plans in your head, it's too easy to lose them amidst all the activity of daily life and work. Writing them down helps you refer to them often to determine your progress and make adjustments as necessary.

In the workplace, written plans serve as documentation of what you expect to and actually do achieve. When working on team goals, writing them down helps all members review the written plans, assure their roles and help each other stay focused on the outcome.

You have several options today regarding where to write and maintain your goals and plans. These options include a notebook, computer file, on a calendar, or in an organized loose-leaf system. Create your own organizer/planning system or purchase one in an office supply store, the stationery department of discount retail stores, or through mail order catalogues. Formal systems are available from Day Timers, Franklin Covey Planning Systems, Priority Management and others.

People who track their time and projects in a formal system are more productive, develop self-confidence and earn respect from others for being organized.

If you question why it's important to have written goals, consider this study conducted at Harvard University in the 1950s. It illustrates the impact of written goals. Graduating seniors were asked how many had written their goals on paper. Only three percent had. Twenty years later, the three percent who had written their goals were worth more financially than the other 97% combined!

Another study conducted in 1979 and 1989 showed that those who wrote their goals in 1979 were earning ten times more in 1989 than those who had not written their goals.

Writing your goals on paper helps you plan how to spend each day. Record both work goals and personal goals to stay focused and create a balanced life. Written goals tell you exactly what you want to achieve and help you allocate your time. When others ask you to do something, looking at your goals and plan helps you decide whether to accept or refuse the request. If you choose to accommodate others' requests, adjust your plan accordingly. Or, if you can't help the person at that time, look at your plan to determine when you will be available to help them.

Set *life* goals first – what you'd like to accomplish in your lifetime. These are very broad and define either what you'd like to be remembered for or what you yearn to accomplish for your personal gratification. Establish *long-range* goals next – what you strive to accomplish in the next 5 – 10 years that will support your life goals.

Then define your *short – range* goals. These cover the coming 1-3 years and support your long-range goals. Set *immediate* goals last – what you need to accomplish in the next few days, weeks, and months to build towards your longer-range and lifetime goals.

Each level of goals supports the next higher level. When you've accomplished the lower level immediate and short-term goals, you will have completed a big part of your long-range and lifetime goals. You'll want to establish new immediate and short-range goals to bring you closer to your lifetime achievements.

After you've written your goals, determine what actions you must take to achieve each one. These actions, called **objectives**, are the tasks, functions, or activities associated with your goals.

Here's an example of my goals. Early in life, I knew that I wanted to help people value themselves and live rewarding lives. In 1989 I realized that I want to make a difference in education and business. I plan to do this by creating a *system* to prepare students for the workplace and help employees develop the skills to build rewarding careers while contributing to their business' success.

I also want to strengthen communication between managers and employees. I believe that managers who recognize employees for their contribution to the business' success build more successful relationships with their staff and the entire company benefits.

These became my professional life goals. To make them happen, I defined and wrote my long-range, short-term and immediate goals.

Two long – range goals that I set in 1990 to help me achieve my lifetime goals are:

1) Design one training program by the year 2000 that prepares students for the workplace and one that helps employees understand business and recognize their value to the organization.
2) Design and conduct a training program by the year 2000 for supervisors on how to coach employees for optimal performance.

Two *short-range* goals that I set in 1997 to support the other goals were to:

1) Complete this book for distribution in September 1999, and
2) Draft a training program for supervisors by October 1999 on "Coaching for Optimal Performance" and, by December 1999, secure at least 5 contracts to present it.

My *immediate* goals to support the above included:

1) Complete at least 50% of the manuscript by April 2, 1999 in order to give my illustrator time to complete his role so we can publish the book by the end of August 1999, and
2) Draft an outline for "Coaching for Optimal Performance" by July 30, 1999.

I exceeded the deadline on the first and completed the second of these goals.

In order to be meaningful, determine *why* a goal is important to you. Knowing why you want to accomplish the goal gives you the impetus to keep going, despite any obstacles you encounter or how weary you may grow at different times during the process.

My goals are important to me because I truly want to help others. I have found that my greatest rewards and satisfaction come from helping others. When I see clients achieve their goals, and they tell me that I've helped them, I feel like I am making this world a better place. This is in keeping with my lifetime goals and supports my values.

Eventually I would like to offer scholarships or start an apprentice program to help others learn about their chosen field. I want to contribute to organizations that help people take control of their own lives and become responsible human beings, accountable for their own destiny.

I believe these programs *will* help students succeed in the workplace and life and strengthen communication between managers and employees. What do YOU want to accomplish and why?

What is driving your desire to do this?

THE DRIVING FORCE (S)

We've already discussed the two emotions that motivate all of us to do whatever we do, and to take whatever action is necessary for completion. These emotions are pleasure and pain.

When you believe that achieving a goal will bring you pleasure, you will work tirelessly towards making it happen. If you believe that you will suffer punishment or embarrassment by NOT achieving the goal, you will strive to achieve it just to avoid the pain.

For example, in school, if you value passing grades and believe that you will fail a class for not completing assignments, you will be motivated to finish the projects assigned to you. When someone hires you to perform a job, they will expect you to perform that job. If you value keeping that job, you will be motivated to do what it takes to keep your job.

Setting goals is more than just thinking about or saying what you'd like to do or have. True goals fully and completely define what outcomes you would like to achieve. Flesh out your goals with objectives that list the specific tasks or steps you will take to achieve your goals. Plans are the written documents that organize your objectives to keep you on target. Plans include the tasks you will perform, the resources you need to perform them, and the timeframe in which you will complete each one. Plans are tools that help you monitor your progress towards achieving your goals.

Effective goals contain specific objectives that tell you exactly what you want to achieve, by when. You can determine whether or not you've actually achieved them. A good model to use when setting your goals is the **SMART** method.

This stands for:

SPECIFIC: exactly what results you want
MEASUREABLE: variables like numbers, colors, size, or brand name that help you determine your progress and how much further you still have to go for completion.
ACHIEVABLE: are within your grasp to complete
REALISTIC: can be completed based on your mental, physical, and emotional abilities and resources
TRACEABLE or TIMEBOUND: list the dates by when you want to achieve each milestone or measure.

For example, one of your personal goals may be to travel. Saying, "I want to travel" is a wish, desire or idea; it is not a complete goal. To make this desire a goal, you could say,

"I *will* travel cross-country by my 25th birthday", or
"I *will* visit three European countries by the time I'm 40", or
"I *will* visit all the continents in my lifetime."
To make these SMART goals you could say,
"I will travel the United States coast-to-coast by bicycle [or car, or train], stopping in at least one major city in each state by my 25th birthday", or
"I will tour Rome, Madrid, and Paris by June, 2031", or
"I will visit the capital region of every nation in Africa, Antarctica, Asia, Australia, Europe, North and South America before I die."

Look at your written goals every day. Your mind will find the time and ways to help you achieve them. You're probably asking why you need to devote time to writing your goals and plans down when you are perfectly happy keeping them in your head. Written goals and plans are like your map for the trips you want to take.

No matter how adventurous you are, you wouldn't set out on a cross-country trip without a map. While a map can't predict *all* of the conditions that you will encounter like weather or road-construction, it does provide the basic direction for you to follow and indicates where some challenges may arise.

A map shows you where the waterways, mountains, and valleys are. It also gives you landmarks so you can track where you are throughout your journey. Knowing this in advance helps you plot your course around the rough terrain. This, in turn, helps you estimate how much time it will take to reach your destination, which, will indicate how much money and supplies you'll need to take with you and what plans you'll need to make in advance for lodging.

Likewise, when you want to achieve a specific goal or objective, knowing where the obstacles or 'roadblocks' are helps you plot your activities and reach your destination in spite of them. Plans also help you see what help you will need from others and what is a reasonable time frame to complete your goal.

For example, your goal and destination in education is graduation. If you decide to go to college or technical school, your goal will be to graduate with a degree in a specific major by a certain date. The objectives in your plan will include:

- Select a major that appeals to you [If you are unsure, a degree in Liberal Arts or Business Administration would be the best major to start with. You can always declare a different major once you have started.]
- Determine how much time you want to take to earn your degree
- Evaluate the pros and cons of a four – year or two – year college or technical trade school.
- Survey different schools to determine which ones offer the program you want
- Decide whether you will commute to a local campus or go further away and live on campus
- Estimate your budget and what options you have to finance your education
- Talk to people who have attended college to get their ideas on what worked for them and what didn't
- Draft a list of schools and evaluate the pros and cons of attending each school on your list
- Apply to schools
- Wait for acceptance letters
- Select the school that you want to attend from those that accepted your application
- Determine what budget you will need
- Notify the school you choose when you will begin attending and obtain all course catalogues for that semester.
- Decide where you will live and research your options.

This completes the first plan that you would create if you plan to attend college.

Once in school, you will need to set other goals and objectives and draft appropriate plans.

- Declare your major.
- Speak with an advisor about the courses you must take to earn your degree in your major.
- Plot out how many and which courses you will complete each semester.
- Generate a list of options in the event that the courses you want aren't offered at the time that you would like or need to take them. [Suppose a specific course that you need to take to graduate isn't offered at the time that you would like to take it. You can look at other colleges that offer this course.]
- Find out if your college will accept credits from other schools that offer the courses you want and need to take elsewhere.
- Determine where to take each program.

Once you've drafted *any* plan, go through each step and ask yourself, "What's the worst that can happen?" Then create a back up plan [Plan 'B'] to address each situation that may not turn out as you expected. These are also called 'contingency plans'.

When you're working on a project in business, your team will have planning sessions to ask questions about what could possibly go wrong with the project. By asking a series of, "What if?" questions, you can plan your actions in the event that the problem actually arises. This way you will still be able to achieve your goals and objective.
Suppose you're planning the company picnic next summer. Some of the questions you'll ask are, "What will we do if it rains?"

Then you could plan an alternate indoor activity in case it does rain, and you'll need to notify everyone of the contingency plan before the actual date of the event.

When you're planning for your education, you'll want to ask yourself, "What will I do if I'm not accepted by my first choice school?"
Or, perhaps the cost of your first choice school is prohibitively expensive but it's where you really want to go. What else could you do to generate the necessary funds? Which other parts of your plan could you modify to still attend the school and earn a degree from your first-choice school?

PLAN, or CHANCE?

Some people are natural planners. They wouldn't think of living a day without knowing what they want to accomplish and how they're going to do it. Others prefer to take each day as it comes and be surprised by what happens.

Without a plan, you could become a victim of everyone else's whims, desires and plans. When you aren't sure of what you want to do, who you want to be, or where you want to go, you'll take the easy way out and let others plan your life for you.

People who live their lives by what others want for them frequently wind up frustrated and unhappy. You'll often hear these people complaining about not having or doing anything they want and not liking life or themselves very much.

These people are always asking, why is life so difficult? If they would only start asking themselves what they would really like to do, and began to plan a way to achieve their dreams, they would find that others will rally around to help them accomplish their plans.

When I was a Director of Human Resources, I interviewed many candidates who didn't know what they wanted to be. I asked them what type of help they needed. Most wanted help exploring different careers and to understand how their education applied to conditions in the workplace.

I realized that I could do something about this. I could apply my experience from Human Resources and training to educate others about the conditions they would find in the workplace and teach them how to prepare themselves for success. Once decided, I drafted a plan to achieve my goals.

I had to leave the corporate arena to achieve my desired results and created a plan to build a business. Personal Growth Systems [PGS] is a service business that helps others succeed in the workplace and life.

I coach individuals on their career plans and conduct training programs to help employees develop the skills to perform their jobs well. In addition to providing services, I also design and sell products – training programs – to help my clients continue their personal and professional growth and development at their own pace.

Now that this book is done, and my training programs are developed, I plan to produce audio cassette and videotape programs to help people learn this material at their own pace that suits their preferred learning style.

My plan includes:

- Writing this book
- Coaching individuals to select a career and create plans to succeed in the workplace and life
- Designing programs for students and teachers about what businesses expect from employees
- Conducting training programs for employees and managers in business to develop skills for optimal performance
- Speaking to business audiences about how to coach employees in the workplace for optimal performance
- Networking with other people who are focused on similar goals and who need the services that I provide.

Based on what other successful people did to build similar businesses, I concentrate on helping others get what they need and want versus worrying about my own. By reducing the worry, I work more effectively and get better results for my clients and myself in the long run.

Setting goals and drafting plans really works. Writing my goals on paper where I can see them every day helps me stay focused on what I want to accomplish. Knowing what I want to achieve has helped me draft long-range, short-term and immediate goals. These help me stay focused on my daily activities.

I regularly meet people who support my vision and offer me opportunities to practice what I do best and love doing – helping others through coaching, training, and speaking. I also meet people who challenge me to look at how I'm conducting my business which makes me think more carefully about the best way to proceed.

When appropriate, I adjust my plans to accommodate the conditions I find. By controlling my own destiny, I no longer fear whether there will be enough money or time for me to achieve my dreams.

Have it your way

You may plan things in advance as I'm suggesting, or you may prefer to adjust to conditions as you go. This works better for some people than for others. One principle of planning and organization applies equally to us all – we *will* achieve what we are sure we want to!

"Successful people move on their own initiative, but they know where they are going before they start"
- *Napoleon Hill*
-

Circumstances may *affect* how you get there but shouldn't determine how you plan to reach your destination. A person who is focused on specific outcomes will find the resources and processes to make his or her dreams come true!

Always remember: *You can be and do anything you want to, as long as you have a plan and remain flexible.*

WHAT SMART GOALS DO YOU WANT TO ACCOMPLISH?

❖ _____

❖ _____

❖ _____

❖ _____

❖ _____

❖ _____

Transfer these goals into a notebook. Then list the activities necessary to achieve each one. After you've written each goal and the associated activities, you're ready to decide which to work on first. We all have the same amount of time each day. How we use it determines whether we create the life we want or fall victim to the whims of others.

Of course there will be times when you will do what others want you to do. In many cases, it will be mutually beneficial to do so especially when helping others also helps you achieve your own goals.

For example, one of your goals may be to obtain a job doing what you love. This will help you to build your career. When you accept a job that someone pays you to do, your work IS your priority, while at work. By performing the activities that the job requires, you will gain the experience and knowledge that help you to build your career. Thus you are helping your employer and also achieving your own goals.

When you do what needs to be done in a timely manner, you will earn the right to be considered for promotional opportunities within the company. You will also become attractive to other companies who need someone with your skills. Doing your job well continues to provide the financial resources that will allow you to work on your other goals outside of the workplace.

When you've written your goals and listed objectives to achieve them, how will you know which to act on first? *Prioritize*, or determine which is the most important to you at this time or stage of your life.

Prioritizing

Prioritizing goals and activities means deciding the order in which you will perform your work. It means choosing one option over others available to you. Choosing one option doesn't mean that you will abandon the others, it just means that you will work on what's most important first. Then, when you've completed your first choice, you can go back to complete the others.

Determine your priorities by identifying your values, beliefs and actions that you deem most important.

Act first on those tasks that satisfy your values to increase your success and happiness.

Values are the things or conditions that are most important to you. Some values that people deem important are achievement, recognition, family, friends, health, independence, and money or wealth. Other values include freedom, challenging work, contribution, leadership, self-respect and open communication.

Set your goals - starting with your life goals. Then create your long, short-term and intermediate goals and objectives. Then assess your values. All of these will help you prioritize which goals to address first.

For example, suppose that your strongest values include belonging, family and fun rather than independence, power and recognition.

You would create and act first on [and choose accordingly] goals that bring you closer to your family rather than on goals that will drive you further away from family. Say you're considering going to college or finding a job right after high school. When you value belonging, family and fun, you would make as your first priority finding a school or job closer to your hometown versus one further away.

This would assure you that you would be around for all family functions. If, however, your strongest values include independence, power and recognition, your goal might include finding schools or jobs far away from home. These would give you an opportunity to develop your independence and earn recognition for taking care of yourself.

When you know what is important to you, select and perform those tasks and activities that will achieve your most important goals.
Prioritize your values and goals to determine which actions to take at what time. And always remember: Grow your dreams, spread your wings and S O A R!

Tips to S O A R [Seize Opportunities And Rewards]

❖ We all have the same amount of minutes, hours, days, weeks and months. No matter how clever, talented or creative you are, you cannot create more time than this.

❖ *Goals* are the specific results or outcomes that you want to achieve or the destination that you want to reach.

❖ People who write their goals accomplish them more than people who carry their goals around in their head.

❖ Pleasure and pain are the two emotions that motivate all of us to do whatever we do, and to take whatever action is necessary for completion.

❖ A good model to use when setting your goals is the **SMART** method.

❖ Prioritizing goals and activities means deciding the order in which you will perform your work. It means choosing one option over others available to you. Start with your life goals. Then create your long, short-term and intermediate goals and objectives.

❖ *Values* are the things or conditions that are most important to you. Choose to act first on those tasks that satisfy your values in order to succeed.

❖ *You can be and do anything you want to, as long as you have a plan and remain flexible.*

Which tips from chapter 6 do *you* value most?
List them here:

According to this, we are right on target for the year...

- CHAPTER 7 -

Like I said...

Hey buddy I'm talking to you!!!

"Brevity is very good, when we are, or are not, understood." - Samuel Butler

Effective communication skills are essential to succeeding in all aspects of life. How you send, receive and interpret information is the key to getting what you want.

In its most basic form, communication is the successful transfer of information from the sender to the specific receiver. You are successful when the message the receiver gets is the same message that you both *intended* to send and actually conveyed.

Communication skills include verbal, non-verbal and written abilities.

Verbal communication deals with words. Skills include speaking, reading and listening. Non- verbal communication is body language.

Written communication is inscribing words on a surface. This can be done manually using pen, pencil, markers or chalk, or electronically via keyboards. Written skills transcribe the spoken word into hard copy so they become transferable or portable.

You may be wondering why it is necessary to develop clear communication skills. Communicating effectively helps you build relationships that affect your success in the workplace and life.

Albert Morabian found that only 7% of our communication is conveyed through the words that we use. A full 38% is conveyed through our tone of voice, grammar, and appropriateness for our audience. The other 55% is conveyed non-verbally - through our facial expressions, hand gestures, posture, attitude and beliefs.

Technology has made the need for effective communication skills more important than ever. You influence others through your spoken, written and implied words. Whether in person, over the telephone, or on - line, your verbal and written communication skills determine your results. You can even control computers with your voice! This makes it increasingly important to communicate clearly and accurately.

Whether you choose to work at an established workplace or from home, you will communicate with others on a regular basis. When you convey your thoughts clearly, people cooperate with you because they understand what you need, want, and mean. Employers cite 'good communication' as the most important skill they seek in employees.

INTENTION

Oftentimes, what you intend to convey through verbal, non-verbal or written means is not what others perceive or receive. Others may interpret your message in a totally different way than what you *intended*. Your intention does not make you a good communicator.

For example, I once left a voice mail message for a colleague that I both intended to be and thought would be received as a compliment. Instead, she was quite insulted. Immediately following a presentation that my colleague made to our employees, I called to compliment her on it. She wasn't in her office so I left a voice mail message telling her what a good job she had done.

If *I* had received such a message from a colleague, I would have been flattered, believing that he or she had enjoyed my presentation and was complimenting me on my delivery. Instead, my colleague heard my message differently. She was quite offended when I said that she "...did a good job". In her mind, I had assumed a role of higher authority and appeared to be evaluating or judging her performance. Since I was her equal rather than her superior, she was offended by my message.

Surprised by her reaction, I asked her how she would have preferred I comment on the quality of her presentation. She said, "By telling me that you enjoyed my presentation rather than passing judgement on the quality of it."

For years I accepted the fact that my colleague and I saw things differently, but still didn't understand why she was offended. A recent experience helped me completely understand my colleague's comments. I reacted to something a new business associate said to me in the same manner that my former colleague had reacted to me.

This new associate observed me conducting a training class and called to give me feedback. She commented first on the conditions of the room where I conducted the class. Although her comments were about the room itself and not my delivery, I *heard* her comments as judgment that I was a less talented trainer than she is.

My feelings were hurt because I thought she was judging my ability and I resented this comment from a peer. Upon examining my reaction, I realized that I allowed my ego to get in the way of clear communication and understanding. Instead of taking time to fully hear her and *respond* to her comments by asking questions to clarify her intent, I *reacted* with an attitude.

We got together later that week to discuss the situation and both recognized that we had misinterpreted each other's comments.

It was a painful lesson for me, but one that I needed to learn in order to recognize how what I had said years ago was the source of pain for someone else. This experience shed new light for me on how to communicate effectively.

Not everyone will react the way that my first colleague and I did in these situations. Most people will, however, snap back at you when they feel that you've attacked them. When you misunderstand how someone reacts to something you say, or you react to something someone else says, look carefully at what's causing the reaction. Examine what role you had in provoking the reaction or response that you receive.

I learned two important lessons from the situations.

In the first case, I learned that people have different perceptions. [You may know something intellectually. You *learn* it when you can relate to it emotionally as well as intellectually.] Just because I wouldn't be offended by something I'm about to say doesn't mean that another person will perceive it the same way.

I first consider how the listener might interpret my message before speaking. Without becoming defensive myself, I select my words in a manner that the receiver/listener is most likely to hear non-defensively.

In the second case, I learned that I'm human. Human nature makes us *react* when we believe we have been attacked or threatened. When we allow our egos to take control, we often perceive innocent comments as threats or attacks.

Knowing this is no guarantee that I will respond perfectly all the time. What is most important is that I am aware of my own behavior and assert myself to clarify any misunderstandings that do occur, so I can rectify them and retain the relationships that are important to me.

REACT or RESPOND

In communication, people either react or respond to the messages that they receive. **Reacting** is considered to be negative communication. You're reacting to a message when you behave in the same loud, harsh or rude manner or tone that you received from the sender.

For example, if someone yells at you and 'gets in your face', you're likely to yell back at him or her and get equally physical. This type of communication is like the type of reaction or combustion that you generate in chemistry class. When you mix two substances [in this case egos and communication styles] that don't blend well, you can create an explosion.

If you feel that someone has attacked or is judging you [aggressive behavior], you're likely to react aggressively, and with hostility. This usually escalates and leads to a breakdown in communication. Reactions normally arise from a battle of wits, when people's egos get in the way of their clear thinking.

Put aside your ego if you want to communicate effectively. Think of your E G O as Ending Good Outcomes or Eliminating Good Opportunities.

Responding is taking the time to recognize your reaction to or your feelings resulting from someone's comments. Think rationally as to the most appropriate way to express your feelings without further damaging the relationship or situation.

When you're honest about your feelings and think about the most effective way to convey your ideas, you will strengthen rather than damage relationships.

Monitoring your words is more critical at some times than others. It's important to think about what you're going to say when you give someone feedback [stating your observations about their behavior] or convey complicated business information.

When someone's performance or technical knowledge is involved, there's a higher probability for misunderstanding and misinterpretation. You'll want to be careful to choose your words carefully.

It's *unlikely,* though not impossible, that someone would be offended during a casual conversation. When you're simply answering a question or voicing your opinion about whom is best qualified to work on a specific project, there's no need to raise your voice, yell, or be sarcastic.

Communicating via e-mail requires more attention to the tone of your message and the words that you use than when you're speaking to someone in person. Written messages are more often misunderstood and misinterpreted. Without the benefit of seeing the reader's body language, it's difficult for you to clarify your intent and rectify the misunderstanding.

When in doubt about how someone will respond to something you are about to say, pause. Tell him or her that you are having difficulty delivering the message and ask him or her how he or she would prefer to receive certain information. By showing the receiver that you're making an effort to communicate clearly, he or she is likely to help you construct the message and will be more open to receiving it.

Instead of assuming that others will automatically understand what you mean, observe their reactions to the spoken and written word. Ask people how they would prefer to receive information instead of blurting out your comments.

Resist becoming paranoid about your communications. Develop an awareness of how others respond to your tone of voice, choice of words, and actions. It's always safe to ask yourself first how someone *might* interpret your comments negatively before saying them.

When you need to communicate with someone in higher authority and are concerned about what or how you will say or write something, ask a trusted fiend or colleague to listen to you or review your memo first.

Watch their response and ask for feedback. If someone is offended by your delivery, watch his or her expression and clarify your meaning if it was misunderstood.

The key to effective communications is to speak or write to *express rather than impress.* Too many people talk just to hear themselves rather to simply convey information to other interested people.

Despite your good intentions, other people will interpret your messages based on their own experience. Differences in communication are just one example of the types of people you will meet in the workplace and life.

DIVERSITY - different ways of communicating

Everyone's mind works a bit differently from others. Communication often reflects a person's values, beliefs, attitude, religion, culture, economic status and experiences. The combination of these variables affects how we interpret what we hear or the meanings that we assign to certain words.

Being different is neither good nor bad, right nor wrong. Different ideas and approaches lead to innovation and often-improved methods for achieving the desired results.

Diversity in the workplace and life is most apparent in our visible differences - age, race, gender, physical attributes and skills. The less obvious signs of diversity include the way we think, our likes, dislikes, experiences, upbringing and preferences for certain jobs or social activities. These all affect the way that we communicate and are addressed in more depth in other chapters.

Our society has coined a term called **WIIFM** [pronounced Whiff 'em] meaning, 'What's in it for me?' This has both positive and negative interpretations.

In a positive sense, when you intend to reach your audience and provide value to *them*, you will speak in ways that show them how they will benefit. You will appeal to what they want and how they like to receive information.

People who truly intend to provide benefit to the listener ask many questions versus speaking at great length. The more you can engage a person by asking them open-ended questions, the better your chance of getting their support.

In its negative sense, WIFFM refers to people who look at any opportunity selfishly, based only on what benefits he or she will personally reap from a situation. If you intend to get the most for *yourself* out of any situation, your comments will reveal your true intention and you'll lose your audience. As soon as they see no value for them in what you are saying, your listeners' minds will drift and they won't hear another word you say.

VERBAL COMMUNICATION – the spoken word

"There is nothing wrong with having nothing to say - unless you insist on saying it." Anonymous

Verbal Communication deals with words, both spoken and written. It includes the ability to speak and read words as well as listen to others' spoken words. Speaking is also referred to as *oral* communication.

The object of speaking is to express one's thoughts and convey information. Good oral communication has a purpose. When communicating orally, you will either initiate conversation or respond to someone else.

You speak to convey information that is necessary or appropriate for your listener or audience to hear. When you speak to hear yourself talk, you are being outspoken. Outspoken people have very strong opinions that *they* believe are valuable to others. Outspoken people are usually so busy talking that they rarely stop to find out if the listener really wants, needs, or is interested in their comments.

Oral communication is informal day-to-day conversations as well as a planned speech when you're making a formal presentation. Day-to-day conversation is unplanned. It is what you say during the course of living, which includes performing your work. This includes expressing your thoughts or ideas, showing interest in other people, or responding to others' questions. In the workplace, daily conversation/communication is a method of obtaining or sharing information that you and your co-workers need to perform your jobs.

More formal speech is called Oral *presentation*. This is usually planned and rehearsed and may be intended for one or more people. We give oral presentations for different reasons.
You may initiate or be asked to give an oral presentation in the workplace or life to:
- Entertain an audience at a special event or function
- Inform your audience by reporting important information about the status of a special project or activity that you are

working on, or educate them to increase their knowledge about a subject.

- Persuade a person or group of people to support your ideas, buy your products or services [as in a sales presentation], or take action [i.e. convince someone to stop smoking and improve his or her health.]

When you give an oral presentation, you expect the audience or listener (s) to do or feel differently about something as a result of your presentation. This action may be unobservable such as being better informed, thinking or feeling differently about a situation than he, she or they did before your presentation. Or, it may be more observable as in taking action on an issue, like voting, performing a task, or changing a procedure in the workplace. Whatever your purpose, you are more likely to get others' buy-in if you consider what *they* need or want.

Good presentations, oral or written, are concise, focused, and clear. They are organized in three components:
1. The opening
2. The body
3. The closing

The opening is your beginning statement - an attention grabber that engages the audience. This is most effectively done with a question, or by stating an interesting fact or statistic.
The body is the bulk of your presentation. Organize your thoughts into three main points. Support each main point with three supporting points. Include some facts, figures and emotional stories to illustrate a point.

Facts and figures appeal to and capture the attention of those who respect logic and analytical thinking. Stories appeal more and will retain the interest of those who prefer feeling [more on this in chapter 8.] Personal stories and examples will reinforce the point you are making to most audiences regarding of their preference for logic or feelings.

Include a transition statement to indicate that you are moving on to your next point. Close your presentation by summarizing the key points you've made.

In essence, during an effective presentation:
* ❖ Tell the audience what you're going to tell them
* ❖ Tell them, and then
* ❖ Tell them what you told them.

I speak to groups of business leaders at Chamber of Commerce meetings. One of my topics is "The Leader in You." My opening statement asks the question: "What trait do businesses seek in employees yet claim they can't find enough?"
The answer is LEADERSHIP.

I tell them I will speak about:

1. What leadership is
2. Why it's important, and
3. How to develop leadership skills in self and others.
For each point, I use supporting facts and comments from recognized experts like Warren Bennis, Peter Drucker, and Tom Peters.

I close my presentation by:
1. Highlighting the essence of what leadership is
2. Citing the benefits they would accomplish for themselves and their organizations by developing these skills, and
3. Stating, "You are great leaders. I know you can do this!

I send them off with the words from my business:
Life is what you make it. Grow your dreams, spread your
wings, and S O A R!" [Seize Opportunities And Rewards]

Think before you speak. Others will listen to you, take your
words and suggestions seriously when they know that you've
thought about them versus blurting them out.

THE FINE ART OF LISTENING

*"A good listener is not only popular everywhere, but after
a while he knows something." - Wilson Mizner*

There are two types of listening, active and passive. Some say
that there is a third type of listening - the non-verbal signals
that we pick up when listening to someone.

Truly listening to another person is an art. We may *hear* the
words that someone says, without really listening to them.

Hearing only the words that someone says is considered
Passive Listening. This is when you hear the person's voice
and recognize that they are speaking, but pay little attention to
what they are really saying. Often times, our mind wanders,
and we are busy thinking about our response rather than
attentively listening to another person.
At other times, we let our personal filters distort what we hear
others say. When our filters are active, we hear what someone
says, as we would like it to be, rather than what it actually is.
OR, we use what is called selective listening, and only attune to
those parts of someone's message that we want to hear or will
accept.

Suppose someone tells you that you aren't any good at a particular skill. Your ego wants to believe that you really are good at it and refuses to hear what the person is saying. Instead of asking what makes the person believe that you aren't good at the skill, your filter shuts out hearing words that you don't like.

Asking questions to understand the nature of his or her comments when someone criticizes us, rather than closing down to their feedback, is active listening. Active listening shows that you have an open mind and are interested in hearing feedback so you can become a better person and perform your job more effectively.

Someone else's opinion of your ability is only that - their opinion. You can only determine if their feedback is valid for you by asking questions to truly understand their concerns.

Truly effective listening is called Active Listening.

Active Listening means that, in addition to hearing someone's spoken words, you can identify the emotion that the speaker is expressing and can almost hear what they mean to say but haven't put into words. When you acknowledge to the speaker that you understand how they feel about a situation, in addition to the words they spoke, he or she believes that you have truly listened to them.

When you paraphrase what someone says to you, and ask questions about what they are feeling or what motivates them, he or she feels like you have fully heard them.

I was listening to a man tell me about a business venture that he had just entered into. When he was finished telling me his

140

story, I told him that I understood he just entered a partnership with another man and was both proud of the accomplishment and concerned about whether it would take up too much of his time. He acknowledged that I had heard more than he realized he said, because he didn't remember *telling* me that he was proud or concerned, but he truly was.

Other ways to indicate to a speaker that you are listening is to occasionally nod your head, smile to encourage them to continue, or softly say m-m-h-m-m-m or uh-huh to indicate that you are following their stream of thought. These subtle tones confirm that you are listening.

Always wait until a person completes his or her thought before cutting them off and finishing their sentences for them. When you finish someone's sentence for them, it usually indicates that you are NOT listening, but are thinking more about what you are going to say. When you are certain that the speaker has completed his or her statement (s), the best way to indicate that you have truly listened is to paraphrase in your own words what you heard him or her say.

True listening, therefore, is hearing the words that a speaker says, *reading* their body language to interpret how they feel about what they are saying, and looking for the meaning inside their words, even if they don't actually say them.

True listening is also waiting for someone to finish their statement before you respond, and asking questions to assure that you understand what they are saying.

NON-VERBAL COMMUNICATION – body language, or what we say without words

"Who you are speaks so loudly that I can't hear the words you are saying" Ralph Waldo Emerson

Non-verbal communication, or body language, refers to our behavior. Behavior is what we do and say. It's what others see us do and hear us say.

Non-verbal communication reveals our feelings, attitudes, beliefs, and values. It's *how* we do and say something. Besides the words themselves [oral communication], non-verbal communication includes tone of voice, speed of speech, and the actions that you take to convey your ideas. Your behavior reflects your attitudes, beliefs, and opinions more accurately than the words you choose to utter.

Remember Albert Morabian's study, which concluded that a full 93% of our communication is non-verbal? This is particularly important when you're communicating on the telephone.

Since only 7 % of your messages come through in your words, the person on the other end interprets your message almost entirely on your tone of voice, speed, gestures and attitude. If you have abundant energy and tend to act and speak without thinking, you may wind up doing and saying things that embarrass you.

You *can* learn to communicate differently and more effectively than you have in the past if you truly want to and believe that you will get better results.

Take responsibility for your communication. Think about what you will say and how you will say it to make sure that what you intend to say is what is actually heard. Be aware of your gestures, facial expressions, posture, speed and tone of voice. You can control these things, which comprise the majority our communications.

WRITTEN COMMUNICATION - hard copy

"Writing, when properly managed, is but a different name for conversation" - Laurence Sterne

Effective written communication refers to your ability to both read and write text. This is critical in the workplace because many of the procedures that you need to follow in order to do your job are written.

You'll need to demonstrate your ability to read and write to graduate from school. In order to get a job, you need to be able to read employment advertisements, look up names and addresses in a telephone book, follow directions to get to your interview, and complete an employment application.

Most organizations rely on the timely and accurate exchange of information to manage their business and serve customers. Systems also rely on accurate and timely data entry to monitor sales activity and track customer orders.
Every company I've worked for requires managers to write monthly reports on their department's activities. In addition, when supervisors appraise employees' performance every year, they often document their evaluations for employee records.

143

Many companies publish newsletters to publicize new products and recognize employees' hard work. Something as simple as knowing how to read your paystub should be reason enough to want to read properly.

Knowing that other employees depend on the accuracy and timeliness of your written results would inspire many people to want to write well.

As in oral presentations, many employees prepare written reports and presentations. The same rules of three apply here as they did in oral presentations.

1. Tell your reader what you're going to tell them - the purpose of your document. [Opening]
2. Tell your reader what he or she needs to know. [Body] (Include three main points with supporting information and clear transitions to the next thought.)
3. Tell the reader what you told them Closing]. Summarize the main points and tell them what action you'd like him or her to take as a result of reading your material. (Recap the document and ask them to act on what you've presented.) [

If you choose to progress to higher levels within an organization, you can count on having to read and write more.

If you are familiar with e-mails and the Internet at home, you will find the same tools used in the workplace. Many organizations have internal networks that include e-mail systems and networks to transfer information. This helps employees at the home office communicate with employees out in the field locations and at other divisions or headquarters.

Smaller divisions must transfer information about their division's activities to Corporate Headquarters on a regular basis. This includes financial information about sales, profits, and expenses.

In chapter two we talked about various functions and departments involved in running a business and providing goods and/or services to customers. How many situations can you identify as a need to write and read effectively?

Suppose you plan to work in a restaurant or auto repair shop. What situations can you think of that would require you to write accurately and clearly?

Look around your daily environment and note how many things require you to read and write. Whatever your need, remember to write clearly, concisely, and to the point. Nothing frustrates people more than having to read volumes of material and not knowing what they're supposed to get out of it.

Preparing good oral and written presentations is much like preparing a good meal for guests. You serve an appetizer to whet your appetite [the opening], the main meal [the body], and dessert [the closing]. If the dessert is good, the entire meal was remembered favorably. If the dessert leaves a bad taste in guests' mouths, they're likely to think that the entire meal was less than satisfactory.

So it is with oral and written presentations. Leave your audience and reader(s) satisfied. You will earn a reputation for being an effective communicator and increase your opportunities for advancement.

Verbal [oral], non-verbal, and written communication skills are essential to succeed in the workplace and in life. Communication is the basis of building relationships as well as understanding and performing the work that you are responsible for in the manner that your employer expects.

Of all the communication skills discussed, listening is considered to be the most important. An unknown author once said, "God gave us two ears and one mouth. Use them in that proportion." This means that listening is more important than speaking if you want to communicate effectively in the workplace and life.

Many factors influence your ability to communicate. Your values, beliefs, attitudes, and experience are shaped by the input you received from family, teachers, and friends growing up. Where you grew up and your socio-economic status also affects your communication skills.

Perhaps the most important factor influencing your communication skills is your behavioral preferences. Psychologist Carl Jung believes that we are born with factors that determine how we prefer to receive and convey information. Read on to learn about his theory and how it affects your life.

TIPS TO S O A R [Seize Opportunities And Rewards]

❖ Effective communication skills are essential to succeeding in all aspects of life. How you send, receive and interpret information is the key to getting what you want.

❖ Your intention does not make you a good communicator.

❖ In communication, people either react or respond to the messages that they receive.

❖ Develop an awareness of how others respond to your tone of voice, choice of words, and actions.

❖ Communication often reflects a person's values, beliefs, attitude, religion, culture, economic status and experiences, which affects how we interpret what we hear or the meanings that we assign to certain words.

❖ Good presentations, oral or written, are concise, focused, and clear.

❖ You are more likely to get others' buy-in if you consider what *they* need or want.

❖ Take responsibility for your communication. Think about what you will say and how you will say it to make sure that what you intend to say is what is actually heard.

What tips from chapter 7 do *you* value most?
List them here:

Verbal, Non-verbal, and listening skills at their best ...

- CHAPTER 8 -

It's a small world after all...
Behavioral Styles and
Interpersonal Relationships

We're all in this together ...

"Today the most useful person in the world is the man or woman who knows how to get along with other people."
- Stanley C. Allyn

Whose way of communicating with others is the *right* way? Each of us believes that our way of communicating and interacting with others is the right way. Indeed, ours is the right way for us to think, act, and behave. The only person that we can truly control is ourselves.

Why do we believe this, how does it affects our lives, and how can this knowledge help us develop behaviors and relationships to succeed in the workplace and life?

BELIEFS

Behavior begins at birth. The very essence of human nature makes us focus on our own needs and wants. From early childhood, we believe that we are invincible and all knowing.

From the moment we are born, we focus on our own needs and wants. When our parents respond to our cries, giving us what we want, we grow to believe that everyone else exists to do what we want, exactly when and how we want it.

We continue through childhood testing this theory that others exist to fulfill our needs and wants. Until we learn that every person feels the same way about him or herself as we do about ourselves, we remain self-centered and create unrealistic expectations of others in the workplace and life.

We trick ourselves into believing that we can control others' attitudes, beliefs, and behavior just by wanting it to be so.

It helps to understand human behavior and preferred styles. Understanding your own and others' behavior helps you build successful relationships in the workplace and life.

At some point, those who succeed in the workplace and life realize and believe that you get more of what you want by helping others get what they want. How each of us comes to this is an individual journey of learning from life's experiences.

BEHAVIORAL STYLES – Why do you do that?

Behavior is what you say and do – your words and actions. Others determine your preferred 'style' by watching what you do and listening to what you say. After observing someone for a while, you can predict how he or she will behave in a given situation.

You are unique ☺. Some things you say or do, and *how* you say and do them, may be similar to other people. Yet your values, thoughts, and unique mode of expressing them is your thumbprint in life. Consider yourself a snowflake! No two are ever *exactly* alike.

Several behavioral scientists have studied human behavior. Their theories, tools, or instruments indicate what each person needs and wants, and how he or she expresses their preferences. By observing others, we perceive what we believe is their personality or behavioral style.

Carl Jung's work greatly influenced Behavioral Psychology'. Jung believed that an individual is born with specific preferences that guide them through life. Two women studied and applied his beliefs to a critical need in society.

Isabel Cook Myers and her daughter, Katharine Myers- Briggs, developed an instrument to determine how a person's behavioral preferences correlates with work that best suits them. Their instrument is called the Myers Briggs Type Indicator ®(MBTI).

It was first used during World War II. Civilians were needed to do the jobs that were created when soldiers went to war. The MBTI® was used to match civilians with jobs best suited to their behavioral preferences.

Since then, the MBTI® has become one of the most widely used tools in career and relationship coaching and counseling. It identifies an individual's preference for four variables:
1. Your source of energy and focus
2. How you perceive the world around you
3. How you make decisions
4. How you act upon your decisions.

How you respond to the instrument indicates how you prefer to behave in various situations. This information indicates how you tend to interact with others and perform in the work place. Knowing your own and others' preferences helps you determine the most effective way to communicate.

It also helps you select the type of job and work environment in which you are most likely to succeed. Before reading about the different behavioral preferences, it is critical to understand some basics:

1. *No* preference is good or bad, right or wrong.
2. Titles used in this instrument refer strictly to a person's preferences and are not intended to box them into categories through labels.

3. Preferences are innate and develop throughout one's lifetime.
4. People may learn about differences and choose to change their behavior, but their preferences remain the same.
5. People who prefer a particular behavior often have difficulty understanding and relating to people whose preferences are different.
6. The following information is intended to give you a broad understanding of these behavioral preferences.

The questionnaire contains four variables. Each variable consists of two choices at either end of a continuum.

When you respond to the questionnaire, your answers indicate your distinct preference for one of each pair. The four choices result in your *preferred* behavioral type. Everyone exhibits some of the behaviors associated with all of the variables, and has a definite preference for four of them.

Myers-Briggs Type Indicator®

Think of yourself as a structure like a silo. Everything within you is Internal. Anything outside of you is External.

The first variable refers to your orientation - where you focus your attention and the source from which you draw energy. The continuum contains a preference for *Extraversion* (E) on one end and a preference for *Introversion* (I) on the other.

People who prefer Extraversion (E) tend to draw energy from and focus their attention on the external world of people, activities, and events. They are called Extraverts. People who prefer Introversion (I) tend to focus on and draw energy from their internal world of thoughts and ideas. They are called Introverts.

Extraverts gain energy from the world around them, rather than what's happening inside their heads. They are more likely than Introverts to talk, seek the company of other people, and keep busy with activities. They gather energy by doing rather than observing things. Extraverts are comfortable in large groups of people and often initiate introductions.

Because they focus their attention on the external world, some Extraverts are considered to 'think out loud'. To fully understand their own thoughts, they need to place them in the external world. Extraverts often clarify their own thoughts by hearing them out loud versus reflecting on them inside their heads.

Introverts gain energy from and focus their attention within themselves. They tend to observe, are often deep in thought and appear to be more reflective than Extraverts.

Introverts tend not to speak often or say much, until they've carefully thought about what they want to say. They prefer one-on-one conversations and may shy away from large groups. Introverts value privacy, their own and others'. Even when asked for their opinion, an Introvert is selective about the people with whom he or she will share their thoughts. When speaking to people they respect about a subject they know well, Introverts can be as talkative as Extraverts.

The second variable is about perceiving - how you gather information about the world around you. One end of the continuum indicates a preference for *Sensing* (S) behavior; the other indicates a preference for *Intuiting* (N).

People who rely on information that they gather through their five senses prefer *Sensing* behavior and are called Sensors. They prefer to give and receive information that is based on what they see, hear, smell, taste, and touch.

Sensors like to receive information in writing. They tend to rely on or are more comfortable with the past than the future. This is because information about the past can be proven. Information about the future is still unknown and can neither be seen, heard, nor touched until it actually happens.

People who gather information without concrete or tangible facts are considered to prefer *Intuiting* and are called Intuitives. Intuitives are more focused on future opportunities and what is possible. They have a vivid imagination and are considered to be creative. Some Intuitives are considered visionaries because they can see what is possible before it actually happens.

Intuitives gather information through their intuition, and what is considered to be the *sixth sense*, or gut feeling. They have such a strong sense of knowing that they often miss important details of a situation.
Thus, Sensors who prefer concrete data and details may perceive Intuitives to be daydreamers and poor listeners who are not based in reality.

Both Sensors and Intuitives are equally sure that their information is accurate and correct. Whereas Sensors can prove their beliefs with tangible facts, Intuitives have difficulty proving their beliefs. They must rely on their powers of persuasion and influence to help others see what they see in their minds.

The third variable, about closure, explains how you reach decisions. One end of the continuum indicates a preference for *Thinking* (T) behavior. The other end indicates a preference for *Feeling* (F) behavior.

People who are very logical and analytical prefer Thinking behavior and are called Thinkers. People who make decisions based on personal values and emotions prefer Feeling behavior and are called Feelers.

Thinkers tend to analyze and evaluate information in order to reach a decision. They reach decisions and evaluate others' decisions based on how logical or how much sense it makes. Feelers tend to evaluate information based on their personal values and the fairness of a situation. They reach decisions based on emotion or how people will feel as a result of a specific message or action. Feelers evaluate others' decisions by the same criteria.

The fourth variable explains your attitude about structure and influences how you act upon your decisions. One side of the continuum indicates a preference for *Judging* (J) behavior. The other side of the continuum indicates a preference for *Perceiving* (P) behavior.

Those who prefer *Judging* behavior like a lot of structure and reach decisions quickly. Those who prefer Perceiving behavior like less structure and prefer to take time to consider various alternatives before making a decision.

People who prefer Judging are usually organized and make plans. They create "To Do' lists to track what they want to accomplish. They also decide, respond and act very quickly when asked to make a choice or do something.

Judging people act very quickly and are comfortable making decisions with limited information. They can appear impatient and impulsive. Because they decide so quickly, some people who prefer Judging are considered to be judgmental.

People who prefer Perceiving like to explore all their options before making a definite decision. They are considered to be open-minded because they are willing to evaluate different possibilities. Because they usually consider several possibilities before making a firm decision, others may view people who prefer perceiving to procrastinate.

*   *   *   *   *   *   *   *

When you complete the MBTI® instrument, your resulting preferences indicate your four-letter *type*. There are 16 possible combinations:

ESTJ ISTJ ESFJ ISFJ ESTP ISTP ESFP ISFP
ENTJ INTJ ENTP INTP ESFJ INFJ ENFP INFP

Each of these behavioral types has specific tendencies that indicate how a person draws energy, gathers information, makes decisions, and acts upon those decisions.

The following word sets are *samples* of behaviors that are associated with each of the variables. The set of words that you relate to most likely indicates your preference.

To determine your true preference, you would benefit by completing the questionnaire. You can obtain it from the website or books listed at the end of this section.

Extraversion (E)	**Introversion (I)**
Interactive	Observant
Easy to know	Hard to know
Multiple relationships	Few close relationships

Sensing (S)	**Intuiting (N)**
Facts	Meaning
Details	Possibilities
Concrete	Abstract

Thinking (T)	**Feeling (F)**
Analyze	Sympathize
Logic	Emotion
Why	Who

Judging (J)	**Perceiving (P)**
Closure	Options
Scheduled	Spontaneous
Fixed	Flexible

Many placement offices or guidance counselors can help you find someone in your community who administers this tool. OR, you can find the Myers-Briggs questionnaire at the following web site:
http://www.onlinepsych.com/public/Mind_Games/ptt/types.htm

You can also find more detailed information about this instrument and behavioral preferences in the following books:
1. "Type Talk" by Otto Kroeger and Janet M. Thuesen; Dell Publishing
2. "Type Talk at Work" by Otto Kroeger and Janet M. Thuesen; Dell Publishing

3. "Do What You Are" by Paul D. Tieger and Barbara Barron-Tieger; Little, Brown and Company
4. "The Art of SpeedReading People" by Paul D. Tieger and Barbara; Barron-Tieger, Little, Brown and Company
5. "Please Understand Me" by David Kiersey and Marilyn Bates; Prometheus Nemesis Book Company

*　　*　　*　　*　　*　　*　　*　　*

SAMPLE DESCRIPTION

My *learned* preferred behavioral style is ENTJ (Extravert, Intuitive, Thinking, and Judging.) My natural preference was ENFJ (Extrovert, Intuitive, Feeling, and Judging). The change from Feeling to Thinking occurred as a result of maturing, gaining additional business experience, and effort.

As an ENTJ, I derive energy by focusing on the external world. I am intuitive, and often see possibilities in a situation before I have all the facts. I'm more interested in whether something makes sense and is logical. I evaluate things more now than I used to, and ask more questions to be sure that my statements make sense to others. When I preferred feeling, I used to evaluate a situation and often made decisions based on my values, whether it *felt* right and was the fair thing to do. My preference for Judging in Myers-Briggs terminology means that I like to organize my work, plan my time, and tend to reach decisions quickly.

I can become impatient and frustrated with situations or people that take more time than I do to reach a decision or take action. Once I realized that the only person whose behavior I could change was my own, I learned to develop patience and

161

more effective communication techniques that reduce my frustration and bring better results.

Though not an easy task, I found the Serenity Prayer a helpful tool in diminishing my frustration and anxiety. It goes like this:
Grant me the patience to accept the things I cannot change
The Courage to change the things I can,
And the Wisdom to know the difference.

As a result, others are more comfortable working with me because I've learned to appreciate each person for who they are, rather than expecting them to behave the way that I would like them to. Now, when someone I work with takes more time than I to reach a decision, I ask him or her how I can help him or her decide. By pointing out the importance of the outcome on the business, together we gather the information they need to reach closure.

My role as a business executive helped me learn and understand differences between preferences. Most of my colleagues and bosses preferred sensing and thinking versus my intuitive feeling. They paid close attention to and preferred detailed factual information. I preferred talking about ideas, possibilities and how fairly a decision would affect the people involved.

For example, when reviewing resumes and interviewing candidates for open positions, I could intuitively feel whether someone would be a good candidate. My boss and colleagues often evaluated resumes and candidates based on the candidate's written and spoken words. As a result, my colleagues and I often differed on which candidates we believed were right for the job.

Sometimes their assessments resulted in candidates who were better suited to the business than the candidates that I favored; sometimes mine worked out better than theirs did. We all recognized the importance of understanding and considering different styles and were willing to support the team's decisions. Rather than pout about not getting my way, I now think about what I've learned from a situation and store the knowledge for the next time I'll need it.

In both the workplace and your personal life, you will find that people who prefer different types of behavior often have difficulty understanding and adapting to people's opposing preferences.

Preferring different behaviors than someone doesn't make either one of you right or wrong, good or bad. Differences in how people think is just another example of diversity.

In effort to serve customers in our rapidly changing world, most business environments prefer detailed, accurate information that can be delivered quickly. Ninety percent of business executives prefer sensing, thinking, and judging behaviors.

You will strengthen your interpersonal skills and build successful relationships when you take the time to understand your own and someone else's preferred behavior style. This increases your effective communication and is more likely to get the results that you desire.

Know when to support your own preferences and when to *adapt* to others' preferred style. Adapting to another's style does not mean giving up the essence of who you are.

YOUR BELIEFS AFFECT YOUR
BEHAVIOR AND RELATIONSHIPS

Your beliefs and expectations about relationships affect how you approach people in the workplace and life. Your beliefs drive your actions, which in turn produce the results that you achieve.

Successful relationships form between people who enter them for valid reasons. In the most successful relationships, each person has:
❖ Healthy self-esteem
❖ Good self- concept, and
❖ Reasonable expectations of him or herself only.

Each believes that he or she has something to offer and does offer their best to others. They are clear about what each person brings to, wants and gets from the relationship. Relationships based on *mutual* attraction, interest, and support succeed.

Unsuccessful relationships result when people enter into them for the wrong reasons or have faulty expectations.
For example, if you believe that you can control others, you will act in a controlling manner. Usually the need to control others masks a person's own insecurities. In reality, controlling people tend to alienate the very people that they want to control.

People who have low self-esteem or lack confidence often enter relationships hoping that another person will make them feel better about themselves. No one can make you feel better about yourself. Only you can make yourself feel good or bad about who you are.

When one person controls the relationship, and another allows him or herself to be controlled, the relationship is bound to fall apart. Controlling people often grow weary of the effort and the one being controlled is bound to resent feeling powerless.

For example, suppose you're attracted to someone who isn't attracted to you. If you believe that you can make them feel the same way about you (control) simply because you want the relationship with him or her, you are fooling yourself. Even if, through persistence, you're able to convince the person to enter a relationship with you, you may find later that it wasn't worth the effort because you wind up doing all the work. Or, you may find that maintaining the relationship requires you to change who you are.

When the relationship turns out not to be what you thought it would be you wind up frustrated and dissatisfied. This illustrates the cliché: "Be careful what you wish for; you're likely to get it." It means that while something may appear to be what you want, you're often dissatisfied with the actual result.

Your beliefs about yourself influence how others see you. When you value yourself and what you have to offer, others will believe in you.

I always believed that my strengths are in helping people develop the skills and confidence to grow professionally and personally. When I worked in organizations where superiors and colleagues saw me the same way, I had opportunities to develop training programs and suggest human resources procedures that remained in place after I moved on.

When I doubted my own ability, my superiors and colleagues doubted me as well. It's perfectly normal to doubt yourself sometimes. When you continuously see yourself as worthless, others will see you the same way and will try to control you in the workplace and life. When you become subservient, trying too hard to please someone, you send messages to your mind that reinforce your negative beliefs.

When you try to change yourself into the type of person that you believe *others* want you to be, you face a losing battle. No matter how hard you try, molding yourself into someone else's beliefs of what you should be or do doesn't work. Any changes you make have to start with your own belief system.

"Inconsistency with ourselves is the great weakness of human nature" - Joseph Addison

The computer term - GIGO: Garbage In, Garbage Out - applies to your beliefs and behavior as well. If you feed your mind negative thoughts [or *accept* other's negative opinions of you], it's difficult to build good relationships. Replace negative thoughts in your mind with positive input on a regular basis, repeatedly. In addition to creating mastery of skill, repetition reinforces the beliefs you need to succeed in the workplace and life.

Recognize that each person in a relationship is partly responsible for its success or failure. Consider the possibility that if the relationship doesn't develop or work, it may be the other person or people involved that chose not to build it with you for their own reasons. When you accept that people do things for their own reasons, you can give up trying to control them, and work harder on developing yourself.

166

RECOGNITION

Human beings want recognition. In the workplace and your personal life, be clear about the type of recognition that you want, and learn to give it to yourself. When you need and expect it from others, you may be disappointed if you don't receive it the way that you desire. Others will praise and recognize you for doing a good job more often when you stop looking for it. Having the self-confidence to acknowledge your own hard work is recognition itself.

Many companies involve employees in making decisions about how to run the business, and reward employees for their good ideas and hard work.

Recognition will come when you understand the company's strategic objectives, and how you help to serve your customers. Accept accountability for the work that you are expected to do. Rather than whine or complain when things don't go the way that you would like, ask questions to find out why. Gather the information you need to improve the situation and take action to make things better.

HOW CAN I USE THIS INFORMATION?

Reviewing this information repeatedly will help you convert it to knowledge. By applying this knowledge to your daily activities, you will build the relationships and career path that help you achieve what you want and gain recognition.

Many people believe that your overall success depends on the relationships that you build in the workplace and life. You've seen how preferred behavioral types affect your ability to build relationships. In addition, recall Maslow's Hierarchy of needs from chapter one. Where you are on the hierarchy at any time affects how you approach relationships in the workplace and life.

Social needs for belonging and acceptance are often satisfied through your involvement with committees or in project teams. While you may form close friendships with people at work, do not *expect* these to fulfill all your social needs. Continue to satisfy them through joining groups outside the work place. Expecting too much from your relationships at work could put a strain on them and affect your ability to perform your job.

You'll satisfy your need for self-actualization when you find your purpose and accomplish what you set out to do in the workplace and life. Your achievements at work contribute to but should not be the sole basis for satisfying this need. Rely on yourself versus others, particularly in the work place, to feel satisfied with your accomplishments.

When you apply your knowledge of behavior in the workplace and life, you will build more successful relationships.

When you ignore what you learn and approach relationships haphazardly, you will likely say and do things that you regret later. Someone once said, "*Choose your words wisely and sweetly. You may have to eat them tomorrow.*"

Human nature tends to make you harder on yourself than others are on you. You'll exaggerate the mistakes that you make and are more likely to ridicule yourself and think the worst, fearful that others are thinking of you equally as badly.

When you commit an interpersonal blunder in the workplace or life, the initial thunder may seem unforgivable at the time. Stay focused on your critical priorities and effective performance. Over time this greatly helps to diffuse the pain from the prior error or ineffectiveness. In a few weeks, days, or even hours, your incident will most likely be forgotten. Effective workers know that it's 'back to business as usual' if the business is to succeed.

Focus on what you do well, versus what you may have done poorly. Learn from the incident and move on. Dwelling on it will only make matters worse. What your mind focuses on expands. If you focus on positive actions, you will return to effective performance quickly. If you focus on the problem, you will repeat it continuously.

Develop a habit of thinking before speaking. This may save you the embarrassment of blurting out something inappropriate. Some people have enormous energy that influences their actions and causes them to speak without thinking.

You'll hear a lot about **teams** in the workplace. Businesses depend on high performing work teams to understand what customers want and assure that the company meets or exceeds customer expectations.

Being an effective team member means knowing what the team is focused on, and doing your part to make sure that the whole team succeeds. Work teams are much like professional sports team where each player knows what his or her role is in helping the team to win.

Building relationships is essential to effective teamwork. With advancing technology, you may be part of a team that is connected via computers. By building effective relationships with the other team members, you will more successfully contribute to the group's effort while reaping personal gratification from the results.

In addition to understanding behavioral preferences and motivating needs, understanding gender differences will help you build successful relationships in the workplace and life.

Many books have been written about how men and women communicate and tend to view relationships.

THE MALE - FEMALE FACTOR

Understanding some basic differences between male and female behavior can greatly affect your success and reduce your frustrations with others in the work place and life.

Understanding these differences will help you recognize the source of frustration you may feel in certain situations. As with the preferred behavioral style information, using this information to communicate effectively will help you build stronger relationships in the workplace and life.

Whether or not you like these statements, accepting them will strengthen your self-confidence by reducing the time and energy you spend trying to change things that you cannot control ☺

The following chart lists broad generalities that reflect my personal observations and research conducted by many other authors. You may be or know someone whose behavior differs from that usually associated with his or her gender. Does your experience support or negate this information? There are exceptions to every rule. The following chart lists differences between men and women upon which most people agree.

MEN tend to:	WOMEN tend to:
Be driven by ego	Be driven by relationships
Focus on one thing at a time	Focus on several things at once
Evaluate their worth by job	Evaluate their worth by Relationships
Speak directly	Speak circuitously
Ask for what they want	Are reluctant to ask for what they want
Tend to talk about themselves	Tend to ask others to talk about themselves
Seek status, independence.	Women seek connection
Men are traditionally protectors	Women are traditionally caretakers
Men need to fix problems	Women vent frustration
Talk about things, events.	Talk about people and feelings.
Give others commands; lead.	Make joint decisions.

TIPS TO SOAR [Seize Opportunities And Rewards]

❖ Understanding behavior helps you build successful relationships with others in the workplace and life.

❖ Adapting your delivery to someone else's preferred behavior style increases the effectiveness of your communication, getting results that you desire.

❖ Your beliefs about your own self-worth affect how you treat others, what you expect from them, and how they will treat you.

❖ Once you accept that people do things for their own reasons, you can give up trying to control them, and work harder on developing yourself.

❖ In the workplace and life, give *yourself* recognition for a job well done.

❖ Human nature tends to make you harder on yourself than others are on you.

❖ Being an effective team member means knowing what the team is focused on, and doing your part to make sure that the whole team succeeds.

❖ Men and women tend to communicate differently.

Which tips from chapter 8 do *you* value most?
List them here:

All for one and one for all...what a team!

- CHAPTER 9 -

Follow the Leader!

80 % of results come from 20% of your efforts...

"No one's a leader if there are no followers."
                              - Malcolm Forbes

Whom do you know that is a true leader? What makes you or
others want to follow this leader?

You are a leader by virtue of your beliefs and actions, not by
your title or desire to be one. To be a true leader, you must *be*
the kind of person, live your life and demonstrate the traits
that make others want to follow you.

In the childhood game, Follow the Leader, one person plays the
leader. Everyone else is a follower and supposed to do *exactly*
what the leader says or does. If you don't follow the leader, he
or she punishes you by putting you out of the game. This is the
leader's way of showing their power, by controlling others.
In the real world, leaders who punish others for not doing what
he or she says, lose their followers and thus are no longer
leaders.

A leader inspires and guides others to do what he or she
believes is best for all involved. Leaders know that you can't
please everyone all of the time and march towards a vision of
opportunity and continuous improvement to benefit the
masses. A leader has a vision of what he or she believes is
possible. Then he or she models behavior that helps others see
the vision, and persists to achieve the dream despite obstacles
or setbacks.

When Martin Luther King told the world that he *had a dream*
where people of all colors would be treated fairly, he set in
motion the wheels to change the way we live. Although biases
and conflicts still exist between people, the world is more open
to equality and receptive to diversity than it was decades ago.

Anyone who desires to achieve great results can do so, as long as he or she has a dream, is clear about the desired results, is willing to do whatever it takes to make it happen and follows through until the dream is reality.

In the workplace and life, any one can exert leadership. Warren Bennis, Dean of the Business School at UCLA says *"leaders do the right thing, managers do things the right way."* There is a difference between trying to get others to do things your way [manage others' performance] simply to prove that you have power, or helping others see how everyone benefits by doing the right thing(s) [leaders].

When the quarterback of your school football team picks a winning play, he doesn't do it just to show off his ability to throw the ball. Other players help to execute the play and the whole team wins.

True leaders display these character traits:
* ❖ Passion for what he or she does,
* ❖ Personal integrity,
* ❖ Knowledge of *self* as well as others, and
* ❖ Effective interpersonal skills.

Leaders truly believe in and are committed to what they do. They take pride in being honest, ethical and moral. Leaders know their strengths and developmental opportunities as well as those of others, and treat people fairly, as they would prefer to be treated.

The Bible gave us the golden rule "Do unto others as you would have them do unto you." International speaker and trainer, Tony Allessandra converted this to the platinum rule, which says, "Do unto others as they would have you do unto them."

178

Suppose you're speaking to someone from a different country. When you deliver a message in their language, you'll get better results than talking in your own language and hoping they'll understand your meaning.

Another true leader in the 20th century was President John F. Kennedy, whose best known comment, "Ask not what your country can do for you, ask what can you do for your country?" inspired people to take action to help themselves and each other. Good leaders make people think for themselves.

When you ask a leader for his or her opinion on a subject, before he or she answers, they will most likely ask "What do *you* think?" A leader helps you to find the answers that are right for you and then supports you in acting on your beliefs.

Leaders help others become the best that they are capable of being. Instead of giving answers, leaders help others find the best answers for themselves. Most of us already know the answers that we seek or we know where to find them. Galileo said, "You cannot teach a man anything; you can only help him find it within himself." And Socrates said, "You cannot teach someone something they don't already know."

Finding your answers requires:

❖ Patience to assess the situation and explore your options
❖ Rational thinking to review the history of the situation, and
❖ Courage to choose and act upon an option.

Talk with others about your ideas. Some may disagree with you and others will agree with you. When you've inspired someone who believes in your dreams, he or she will ask how they can help you. The more people supporting your ideas, the better the likelihood that your vision will become a reality.

When selecting a focus for Personal Growth Systems, I observed what people are drawn to today. Knowing that people want to succeed and will only grow and change when they deem it necessary and valuable, I decided to focus on the power of choice and purpose. Thus, Personal Growth Systems is about Transformation on Purpose! My coaching, training, and speaking engagements are all about helping people discover how to succeed in the workplace and life. I am just the conduit to making it happen. My clients, students and audiences do the actual work.

It may *seem* easier to simply ask someone else for answers to something that's puzzling you. Unless he or she is the *only* person with the information you need, it could appear that you're looking for an easy way out rather than exerting a little effort. You can lead yourself to the answers you need.

Think of how proud you feel when you've taken time to think about and obtain answers that you need for yourself and then have the courage to apply your knowledge. When others recognize that you're a thoughtful and resourceful person, they are more likely to believe in your ideas, support your efforts and help you achieve your objectives.

"A man who wants to lead the orchestra must turn his back on the crowd." - James Crook

A good leader is curious and will take risks to achieve his or her vision. He or she isn't concerned about whether others think that he or she is doing the right thing.

The leader says WHAT outcome is possible. Then he or she focuses on achieving the desired outcome. This focused vision and behavior inspires others who believe in and also want to achieve the desired results. Despite what others may initially think of the leader's dream, when he or she believes fully in the possibility, the leader will act to achieve that dream. Leaders will do what others won't so they may have what others only wish for.

I was hired as the Director of Human Resources in private industry to improve the Human Resources function. My first project was to improve our recruiting process. Before I was hired, positions were often vacant for several months because of the volume of work that the Human Resources staff was handling. This delay in filling open positions meant lost revenues. I improved the process and shortened the amount of time that it took to fill open positions, especially in the Sales department.

I interviewed and evaluated the recruiters and the process that was used to find candidates before I was hired. When they failed to produce the results we desired in a timely manner, I identified additional resources, focused on colleges, and drafted a new procedure to consider existing employees for open positions. Thus we improved the procedure for hiring new candidates and were able to promote more employees.

Rather than destroy the company's existing relationships with recruiters, who had found us candidates in the past, I expanded our resources and options to generate additional candidates. In revising the staffing process, I was able to negotiate better fees with new providers, thus improving the company's cash flow. Other divisions adopted this new recruiting network and procedure, which strengthened the pool of available candidates throughout the organization. Some of my colleagues questioned my ideas at first. However, I persevered, and continued to show them how we would all benefit from the new process.

The former process required us to hire sales representatives who had prior experience in direct sales of a tangible product. The new process resulted in our first hire of a student graduating from college who lacked this specific experience. Burley Clark joined our company as Inside Sales Representative in October 1994.

Burley's energy, enthusiasm and pride in his accomplishments impressed me during our telephone interview. I saw that he had a vision of what he wanted to do with his life and was willing to work hard to achieve his goals. Burley had a passion for sales. He financed his college education by working two jobs while attending school. This demonstrated his results-orientation and willingness to work hard. During our face-to-face interview, Burley's clear focus on and ability to express what he wanted to accomplish convinced me that he would be a great asset to our team. I immediately recommended that we hire Burley.

In order to gain my colleagues' total support, I reminded them of the difficulty that we'd been having finding qualified candidates for this position. We finally agreed that the sales we were losing with the position vacant cost us more than offering Burley (an unknown) an opportunity to show us what he was capable of achieving. To my great relief [but not surprise], Burley did everything he said he would, and more!

At times Burley needed coaching and feedback from his supervisors and the management team. As he was learning his position and the company, he needed information to accomplish what we all wanted. We supported his ideas and provided the resources he needed because he demonstrated how his ideas were in the best interest of all involved. When a company succeeds, all employees share in the success.

Burley's dream is to someday become the General Manager or President of a division for a large company. Some executives were concerned that his ambition and self-confidence might alienate others and be viewed as lacking maturity or business savvy. Fortunately, customers viewed Burley's enthusiasm as a deep desire to help them. He always looked for opportunities to learn the business, serve the customers and progress into more responsible positions. As a result, Burley was promoted faster than anyone else in the company, just seven months after coming to work for us.

Some of his colleagues envied Burley's quick progress, yet few of them asked for the help that he did to earn the recognition he received. It turned out that his colleagues admired his success and enjoyed working with him because he believed that *together* they would accomplish great things. Burley inspired others to work harder too. He is a true leader who discovered the value of helping others determine what to do for their own growth and goal achievement. In four years, he was promoted twice, won major sales awards and was selected to travel to Germany to teach employees in another division how to sell their products effectively.

Just before I left the company, Burley told me about his idea to create a new position in the Sales department. He believed that if he spent half his time selling to customers and half his time training sales representatives, the company would benefit from increased revenues and a stronger sales force. It would also give Burley the experience supervising others that he knew he needed to grow towards a management role.

We discussed what he would need to consider and the best method of conveying his ideas to senior management. Based on our discussion, he needed to show that the benefits would outweigh the increased expenses of his travel and time out of the territory. Burley created a plan to show management how creating this new position would generate additional revenues and decrease turnover - both benefits to an organization.

Shortly after I left the company, Burley succeeded in gaining management's approval and is living his dream job, on his way to greater opportunities in the future.

"A true leader has the confidence to stand alone, and the compassion to listen to the needs of others. He does not set out to be a leader, but becomes one by the quality of his actions and the integrity of his intent. In the end, leaders are much like eagles...they don't flock; you find them one at a time." - Anonymous

LEADERSHIP STYLES

True leaders have a strong sense of who they are, and demonstrate their values and beliefs through their actions. In business and life, you will discover people using different leadership styles. People usually follow a leader whose vision they support and whom they respect, trust, and admire as a person. Followers determine which leaders they want to follow based on how the leader treats others. Here are some styles that you may come across or choose to use yourself:

The **Autocratic** leader exerts high control over and imposes his or her decisions on followers rather than guiding followers to make decisions for themselves. This leader tells others what to do, and often manages by intimidation or fear that going against his or her direction will result in painful consequences.

A **Benevolent - autocratic** leader may be friendly and kind to workers, asking them for input, but ultimately believes that s/he knows what's best for the organization and thus tells followers what to do.

The **Coaching** leader helps employees discover their own answers believing that followers/employees who work on their own development will achieve greater results for the company. He or she focuses on the future and asks questions to help others create and execute plans for *their own* growth and development.

A **Consultative** leader solicits and applies followers' suggestions on how to achieve desired results. He or she offers suggestions when asked for them or poses suggestions as questions to help followers reach their own conclusions. For example, rather than tell somewhat what to do, a consultative leader will say, "Have you considered...?", or "What do you suppose might happen if you tried...?" This helps the follower create his or her own decisions and choose which actions to apply.

The **DEMOCRATIC** leader believes in the group's abilities to make decisions and achieve results. He or she treats others as equals, participates in the work with them, and may defer decisions to the entire team.

According to Warren Bennis' description of managers and leaders, managers do things right while leaders do the right thing. This means that managers make sure that employees perform their jobs according to company expectations. Leaders believe that by telling employees what the company expects to achieve, they will operate in a manner consistent with the organization's values, beliefs, goals and objectives. Oftentimes, this means leading yourself to do the right thing, consistent with your goals and values.

"People don't want to be managed, they want to be led"
- Dana Conover

When I met Dana, he had just left his job as Marketing *manager* for a well-known company. He intuitively knew that his leadership talents weren't recognized in the company. He wanted to run an entire marketing function and knew he had to search for opportunities elsewhere. Dana's diligent research and networking led him to a position as the *Director* of marketing for a company that markets Warner Brother figures internationally. As a result, he moved to Florida, bought a beautiful new home, gets to travel to exciting, fun-filled places and spends every day doing something he loves with people who appreciate his talent and leadership. Dana grew tired of being told he couldn't lead, and led himself to his ideal job.

Human nature resists being told what to do. Leaders recognize others' need and desire for independence and help their followers discover the path that's right for them.

Do you have what it takes to be a leader? Be honest with yourself on the leadership assessment. Tally your results to determine whether you currently have a leadership attitude.

ASSESSING MY LEADERSHIP POTENTIAL

	USUALLY	*SOMETIMES*	*RARELY*
1. I look for the positive in times of change	☐	☐	☐
2. I'm willing to take risks and learn from my mistakes	☐	☐	☐
3. I regularly acknowledge others' accomplishments	☐	☐	☐
4. I reflect the values that I believe in.	☐	☐	☐
5. I look for ways to share power and credit.	☐	☐	☐
6. I delegate tasks with authority and decisiveness	☐	☐	☐
7. I have written goals and am committed to them.	☐	☐	☐
8. I know what motivates other people and encourage them to be self-motivated.	☐	☐	☐
9. I make decisions in a timely manner.	☐	☐	☐
10. I regularly give honest, constructive feedback to others.	☐	☐	☐

Give yourself 1 point for each question that you answered 'Rarely', 2 points for each question that you answered 'Sometimes', and 3 points for each question that you answered 'Usually'.

If your total is between 10 - 12, you still have much to learn about being an effective leader. People who follow you may do so out of fear or obligation, but rarely will voluntarily support you in achieving your vision.

If your total is between 13 - 23, you have learned and exhibit many of the qualities of a leader. Followers will start to listen to your ideas and may stay with you long enough to see what results you achieve.

If your total is between 24 - 30, you clearly understand and exhibit the qualities of leadership. Others want to work with you, believing that they will be better people for knowing you.

To develop your leadership traits, read more books and observe others whom you deem to be leaders. Ask them what they did to develop leadership traits and whether they'd be willing to help you do the same. A leader who agrees to help you do this will be your *mentor*.

A mentor is someone who is very knowledgeable about his or her business and teaches others how to succeed in that environment. Many companies offer formal programs on mentoring for employees who are deemed as highly promotable and exhibit leadership potential.

You may be assigned a mentor, or seek one for yourself. Search for someone who is well connected throughout your organization, knows who to go to for support, and has access to resources to achieve his or her as well as the company's goals and objectives. A mentor may be your superior or peer. You'll know that you're highly regarded in your company when others ask you to mentor them or senior management asks you to mentor others.

THE LEADERSHIP ROLE

When you're a leader, others will automatically believe that you have certain authority, power, and responsibility. This can help you accomplish your goals and make your vision reality if you use these traits effectively. If you abuse, threaten or punish others, you may not be allowed to continue in the role that brought you the authority, power, and responsibility in the first place.

Authority is having the power you need to carry out your responsibilities.
Responsibility is something that you are held accountable for. In the workplace, the higher the level of your position, the more responsible you are to assure that employees in your department produce the results that help the business succeed. You will have to explain to senior management when your department's work is late or of poor quality. As a leader, you inspire your employees to perform their jobs because it's the right thing to do, and will benefit everyone in the end.

In your personal life, you may assume a leadership position in an organization or club group. If you are captain of a sports team, president of a fraternity/sorority, leading a scouting troop, or playing Big Brother or Sister to a younger child, you will be responsible for carrying out the tasks that you've committed to.

Others will see you as having power when you are authorized to carry out your responsibilities and lead others towards achieving business goals. *Power* may be seen as having and exerting the right to control others. Just as leaders need followers, power is only useful when others recognize that you have it and are willing to follow you when you exert it.

There are several different types and sources of power. Regardless of your role in the organization or group, you may possess or have access to others who possess power to help you accomplish your objectives. Some specific sources of power include your:

1. title
2. appointment to a specific job
3. ability to reward or punish others
4. persuasive ability [communication skills]
5. personal influence [whom you know and can get to help you or your team]
6. knowledge and technical skill
7. skill or ability to perform and achieve results
8. personal charm/charisma

These types of power fall into seven categories. Recognize what it is so you'll know how to handle yourself when faced with it rather than remembering each category.

A. <u>Legitimate or Position Power</u>: says that the higher your level in an organization, the more power you yield over those in lower levels in the organization. The CEO and President can approve or veto what the Division Vice Presidents & General Managers do. A supervisor may discipline an employee who is abusing resources or privileges. A team leader may become the group spokesperson.

B. <u>Reward Power</u>: allows the leader to reward a follower for his or her actions. The value of the reward varies by the receiver's perception. Some employees value verbal praise as a reward, others only recognize a bonus or tangible award as sign of approval.

C. <u>Coercive Power</u>: is the ability to punish others and is based on fear. Used extensively, this causes resentment and dysfunctional performance by the followers.

D. <u>Connection Power</u>: refers to whom you know. Often called 'politicking', this power implies that you can get things done simply because those you know are willing to help you.

E. <u>Expert Power</u>: is technical expertise or knowledge about a product, procedure, activities or issues that are considered powerful.

F. <u>Charismatic Power</u>: refers to someone's personal qualities and how others view them. It can help you influence others over whom you have no control or other type of power.

G. <u>Information Power</u>: like connection and expert power, refers to an individual's ability to access and convey information about particular issues or activities, regardless of one's position.

People who truly have power and want to be seen as leaders usually don't boast or brag about their power. They just use it quietly to obtain the support and resources they need to achieve their vision, and help others to grow. Like it or not, power and politics are part of every organization. Whether or not you use these strategies, it's helpful to recognize what they are and when they're being used against you.

To develop your own power:

1. Network with influential people.
2. Do something to help others.
3. Develop and share your expertise/knowledge.
4. Perform your job well and earn seniority.
5. Be distinctive and recognized for it.
6. Build your good reputation slowly.
7. Help your boss succeed.
8. Speak well of your company to others.
9. Volunteer for assignments.
10. Use praise effectively.
11. Laugh with, not at others.

Let your performance show others what you are capable of, not just because you say so. Show people through your actions that you are willing to help them. Actions do speak louder than words. When you share your successes with others, you will be asked to do more which increases your success and pride of accomplishment.

The longer you stay with one organization, the better known you will be. If you have a specific talent, knowledge or skill, suggest to your supervisor ways that you can apply it to the company's benefit.

Be patient with the changes that you suggest. It takes time for people to earn other's trust and respect. If you try to do it too quickly, people may wonder what you're trying to cover up. You've heard the cliché, it seems to good to be true. This holds for reputations as well as offers for commercial deals.

When you work hard to help your boss [and colleagues] achieve mutual objectives, you will earn the reputation for being a team player, focused on company success.

You may have heard the expression, "Don't bite the hand that feeds you." When you are recognized in your organization, speak well of it to others. New employers will look upon you more favorably when you speak well of past experiences. Speaking ill of your past experiences will make others wonder what you're going to say about them behind their back and they may be reluctant to hire you. No employer wants to knowingly hire someone who will spoil others' morale with tales of woe from the past.

The *best* way to demonstrate your initiative, get opportunities to learn new skills, meet new people, and develop your leadership qualities is to volunteer for new assignment. In turn, this will help you gain the support you need for a project that you create and will increase your visibility.

Always be sincere when praising others. Be specific about what he or she did that you appreciated and why it is valuable. Charles Schwab, founder of the financial institution bearing his name, earned his first million dollars at age 38. When asked for his secret, he said, "...the ability to arouse enthusiasm with appreciation and encouragement" helped him grow his empire. He found that one of the secrets to good relationships and successful business was to praise employees.

193

He advised others to "...be lavish in and anxious to praise others and loathe to finding fault". It is often the easiest concept to grasp and yet the most difficult to perform... treating the other person as the most important.

No one likes to feel foolish. When someone does something that you find humorous, be kind in your words and deeds. Refer back to Charles Schwab's advice above. Most importantly, learn to laugh at yourself when you've made a mistake. You will increase your reputation as a leader when you can take mistakes in stride and see them as learning experiences.

Following these guidelines will likely help you develop the leadership presence that you desire. There *is* a leader in you! Discover your passion and make a commitment to improve conditions for you and others.

TIPS TO S O A R [Seize Opportunities And Rewards]

- ❖ No one's a leader if there are no followers.

- ❖ Leaders do the right thing, managers do things the right way.

- ❖ A true leader displays passion for what he or she does, personal integrity, knowledge of *self* as well as others, and effective interpersonal skills.

- ❖ Leaders help others become the best that they are capable of being. They help you find the answers that are right for you and then support you in acting on your beliefs.

- ❖ The more people you have supporting your ideas, the more likely that your vision will become a reality.

- ❖ A mentor is someone who is very knowledgeable about his or her business and teaches others how to succeed in that environment.

- ❖ A good leader is curious and will take risks to achieve his or her vision and isn't concerned whether others think that he or she is doing the right thing.

- ❖ Regardless of your role in the organization or group, you may possess or have access to others who possess power to help you accomplish your objectives.

- ❖ True leaders don't boast or brag about their power. They use it quietly to obtain the support and resources they need to achieve their vision, and to help others to grow.

Which tips from chapter 9 do *you* value most?
List them here:

Follow your goals to your dreams ...

- Chapter 10 -

Like it or not...Understanding office politics, Networking and Adaptability

Yes you *can* teach an old dog new tricks ...

"You can easily judge the character of others by how they treat those who can do nothing for them or to them."
Malcolm Forbes

We learn in life that we won't like everybody. And that's okay. In our personal life, we can choose most of the people with whom we associate or build friendships. In the workplace, we may get to choose whom we work for and with, but cannot always choose the people who become our colleagues, superiors, or subordinates.

You will work with some people whom you won't particularly care for. You will, however, be expected to work with these people effectively, as a united team. This chapter explores the concept of Office Politics, Networking and the critical skills of Adaptability and Flexibility.

It helps to know about corporate or office politics simply because it exists. There is an expression that says, "Forewarned is forearmed". If you're aware of what you may encounter, you will be better prepared to handle these situations when you face them.

Corporate or Office 'Politics'

This term refers to conditions in an organization regarding communication and power. Politics in business closely follow the structure that we see in the political structure of our government. In government, the amount of power and authority that politicians have depends on what office they hold and in which jurisdiction they hold it.

In business, the amount of power and authority that employees have depends on their position and title and the level where that position sits on the organizational chart. In addition, company policies and procedures dictate who is *accountable* for directing, managing, and controlling others.

Although private citizens elect many government politicians, several positions at the local level are filled through appointments. This means that a person with higher authority selects whom he or she wants to fill positions within their span of control.

The same is true in businesses. Stockholders [who own pieces of a big corporation] vote for and elect the people that they want to serve on the Board of Directors [the highest level within a company]. The Board of Directors determines who will fill the senior management positions in the corporation.

Each level of management then interviews and selects the people who will occupy the positions at lower levels in the organization. The amount of power and authority that you have in an organization depends on your title, level, span of control, and ultimate responsibility.

The term 'corporate politics' frequently connotes a negative culture and uncomfortable atmosphere at work. This is because employees often feel that an employee was appointed to a position based on personal connections and not for his or her abilities. Many employees feel like management is playing favoritism when evaluating and selecting employees for promotional opportunities.

Just like politicians in the public sector are often accused of saying anything that voters want to hear in order to get elected, *politicians* in the workplace are often accused of building relationships with people at higher levels in their organization for the sole purpose of getting what they want.

You may have heard the cliché, "It's not what you know but who you know that counts". This refers to knowing people who have the power and authority to allocate resources, effect changes, and appoint you to a position that you may want to occupy.

From its negative perspective, politicians in government and business appear to exaggerate their own worth and make promises that they neither intend to nor are able to keep. They may also be seen as 'pushing their own agenda' versus looking out for others' best interests.

From its positive perspective, in government and business, knowing the right people can often help you get what you want or accomplish what you need to do.

For example, state politicians appoint or recommend students who are accepted into military colleges. Suppose that you want to attend one of these schools, and your parents are friends with a state official. The connection or friendship *may* help you get into the school that you desire. It's no guarantee, but it's a good place to start. Some people believe that awarding you favors is unethical or inappropriate.

Regardless of whom you know, you'll need to earn an endorsement, appointment, or promotion based on your own merit and worthiness for the appointment.

Knowing the people who make important decisions gives you an advantage over others in that it helps the decision - makers evaluate your qualifications. While you may not always like these conditions, you would be wise to acknowledge that they exist and work within the system rather than trying to buck it.

In the business setting, you will encounter people with similar abilities to help you. If a new position opens up that you would like to apply for, knowing the people who will select the person to fill that position will help your cause. It won't guarantee your selection. You must still earn the promotion or appointment by demonstrating a track record of quality performance and possess the competencies that are likely to add value to the new organization. Politics in the workplace refers to the organizational structure or hierarchy in a firm. Those in higher levels of the company have authority over those at lower levels in the company. Business politics means knowing who you can/should speak with in the proper sequence about a given situation, and adhering to the company's policies and procedures.

From a positive perspective, 'politics' help you achieve the results that you need to. For example, if your boss is well respected in the company, he or she can clear the path for you to get the resources you need to complete your project.

If you work for someone who is not well respected in the company, the fact that you work for that person could inhibit the resources the company will allocate to your project. In order to take action on some of your ideas, it is important that you speak first with your direct supervisor. If you have a question, especially if you dislike something, and go the your supervisor's supervisor, or higher, you could be viewed as disrespectful or arrogant. You will certainly be viewed as inappropriate and may receive a reprimand or discipline.

Mistakes in politics can damage your reputation in the workplace, which can damage your self-confidence.

Remember the example of the employee who learned that a new division is being formed in his company? He called the Vice President of the new organization to tell him how interested he was in working for him. When the employee's boss and Vice President in his current organization found out that he'd gone directly to the management in the other division without first consulting them, they became angry.

They were concerned because he failed to follow protocol [established procedures] and viewed his action as selfish, not having the best interest of his current division in mind.

Take the same situation with a slightly different twist. Instead of you initiating the contact with another division, one of their managers contacts you, without having gone through the proper *chain of command* in advance. You're flattered by the interest, and agree to meet with the other division. You forget, however, to tell your supervisor about the contact. When he or she learns about it from the other division after the fact, many tempers could flare. You could wind up losing the opportunity without ever knowing why and damage your credibility in the process.

Most organizations have a protocol for considering internal employees for new positions. Usually the Vice Presidents discuss their needs with each other, and ask their Human Resources staff to identify candidates whom they believe are qualified for the position.

If your name comes up on the candidate list, all appropriate parties must agree to your qualifications and readiness to be considered for a promotion, Then you will hear about it directly from your Human Resources staff or immediate supervisor. When staff members or employees ignore this practice and take matters into their own hands, the parties involved lose trust, respect and confidence from their peers and other levels in the organization. If you're involved in the misunderstanding, you may be disciplined or lose out on other future opportunities.

When someone in another department or division offers you an opportunity or asks you to do a special project for them, make sure you know what is involved and how much time it will take. Then ask the person who contacts you if they have spoken to your supervisor or division management about the offer or issue.

In many companies, supervisors are expected and authorized to assign work to their own employees. You are expected to ask a manager who wants you to do something for his or her department to see your supervisor for approval.

The exception to this rule is when you are working on a team project where one manager/supervisor is authorized to distribute work to team members, regardless of which department or division they come from. In any case, keep your manager/supervisor informed about your business activities.

Politics appear to be more visible and difficult in small companies than large companies, because most employees know each other. There are fewer employees in small companies and more competition for the rewards to be won, so the politics are obvious.

Politics are widespread in large companies, but the individuals who engage in them may not be as noticeable because of the vast number of employees.

The cardinal rule in dealing with office politics is to be aware of them and keep your wits about you. Do the job that you were hired to do in the best manner that you possibly can. Remain honest and treat others professionally. Ask your peers, colleagues and supervisor what the appropriate protocol is for obtaining and sharing information.

You may not be able to avoid office politics, but you can do your best not to make matters worse. Burying your head in the sand and pretending that these conditions won't exist will not help you succeed in the workplace of life.

When done with the intent to *help* others versus only looking out for one's own benefit, office politics relates to a very favorable process called **Networking**.

NETWORKING

Networking is meeting people to share information that helps each other achieve goals and objectives. It occurs in your professional and personal life. Networking is your *conscious* and intentional effort to meet others in order to expand your resource bank.

The term networking comes from the computer industry. A computer network is the connection between mainframes and Macs or personal computers. The network exists to make information easily accessible and transferable to people who need and want it. The largest computer network that we see today is the Worldwide Web and the Internet.

A people network is all of the people that you know. It starts with your family, relatives, friends, teachers, and neighbors. As you move into the workplace, your network will expand to include the people with whom you work in various companies and the jobs that you occupy. It also includes all of the customers, suppliers, vendors, etc. that you come in contact with in the course of doing your job.

Once you meet someone, he or she becomes a member of your network. You can build a permanent network by keeping a list of names, addresses, and telephone numbers of the people you meet.

Make note of what kind of work they do, what interests them, and the things that they want to accomplish. Then contact them periodically to keep your relationship active. You might send them articles, news announcements, or call them with items of interest to them or help them achieve a goal or objective.

For example, note the teachers and professors that you've had in your education. As you come upon magazine articles that pertain to their subject, send them a copy or call them to tell them about it. Stay in touch with former classmates and colleagues. Then, when you need to find an expert in a particular field, you will most likely know someone in your network that can help you with whatever you're trying to accomplish.

Suppose you want to study law. Start networking by asking your family, friends, and neighbors what lawyers they know.

Be sure when you contact the lawyer(s) they refer you to, that you tell them who referred you to them. Ask his or her advice on what lawyers do and what you need to know and do to become one.

He or she may recommend a good school to you, and may even refer you to their firm or others for intern work and a potential job when you obtain your degree and pass the bar exam.

Or, you may be interested in playing a musical instrument for a band. Asking your network for a good music instructor will get you started. It may lead to opportunities for your band to obtain some bookings. Once you are a member of a band, contact the people in your network to find other people who are interested in using a band for their family or business parties, events, or affairs.

You may decide that you would like to work a particular company like Microsoft. Ask whomever you know who *they* know that might be able to put you in touch with someone at Microsoft. Even if someone doesn't personally know of someone that can help you, just asking the question will stimulate their thinking and give you suggestions that you didn't think of on your own.

My book illustrator used networking effectively to pursue one of his dreams. Jason Greene designed a logo that he wanted to sell to clothing manufacturers. He asked me whom I knew in the New York garment industry that he could contact about his design.

I didn't personally know anyone. I do, however, know several people who either live or have lived and worked in New York - the center for the garment industry. I sent an e-mail message to all of my friends and colleagues, asking who they knew that could help Jason with his idea.

One friend in New York referred me to *his* friend who works for a major clothing manufacturer. He agreed to meet with Jason and gave him several contacts and ideas for licensing his designs. You may already be familiar with ASKII® clothing, which displays a hangtag that says:
"What are you smiling at ☺?"

In addition to referring me to someone in the garment industry, when my friend found out that Jason is a gifted artist and web designer, he asked if Jason would be willing to work with him on his website.

The best way to keep your network alive is to do things for them. They will always be there for you when you need information or a favor. One way that I keep my network active is to inform people about books, audiotapes, workshops and conferences that I believe would interest them. By offering them items of interest, I find that people gladly refer business opportunities to me or share information that helps me with my work.

You will naturally stay in closer touch with some of the people in your network than others. It makes good business and personal sense, however, to touch base with everyone in your network periodically. This builds mutual interest, keeps you current on what's happening in others' lives, and reduces the chance that people will think or feel like you're taking advantage of them.

Like everything else in the workplace and world today, your network will constantly change. It will expand and grow as you continually meet new people. And, when you or others move, you may lose touch with some people. Keep your network, like your attitude, flexible and adaptable to the changing needs and conditions in your workplace and life.

ADAPTABILITY and FLEXIBILITY

"The world hates change. Yet it is the only thing that has brought progress." - **Charles F. Kettering**

Welcome the changes that occur in your workplace and life. Change signals new opportunities and possibilities. If you fear change because of the unknown, you may pass an opportunity to do and be everything that you want. Become involved in the process so you feel like you can control what is happening to you.

The opposite of adaptable and flexible is rigid and unyielding. If you must always have things your way, you will encounter much frustration in the workplace and life. Recognize that having and voicing your opinion is not the same as insisting that yours is the only right way to do something. We often learn a good deal about ourselves by listening to others' points of view.

How many times has someone suggested that you taste a new food or go to a certain movie and you refuse because you believe you won't like it? Many times, once we agree to taste the food, or see the movie, we wind up really enjoying it and wondering why we made such a fuss in the first place.

210

Suppose that, as a toddler, you gave up trying to walk because your first steps were unsuccessful and you believed that you'd never master the technique. Where would you be today?

In the workplace and life, you will be asked to do new things or try different methods to perform your job. Or, changes may occur in the business that require you to adapt to new things and techniques. When businesses re-organize or merge with other businesses, the management staff may change. You may be asked to move to another part of the country or deal with people who speak a different language than you do. The possible changes are endless and often are things over which you have no control.

Human nature is to resist change. The human mind is also trainable and can learn to adapt to many situations. You will find that, adapting to changes and being flexible in your approach to different situations will earn you a reputation of being cooperative. When you resist and complain about changes that occur, you will earn a reputation for being difficult

Why not make change a game? Become the first to adapt well to changing conditions. See what opportunities are presented and develop a reputation for leading others to better methods and techniques of dealing with the change.

One of the most important aspects of the workplace where you need to be flexible is the issue of compensation. Too often we decide what we are worth, and refuse to accept a salary that is less than that number in our head. That is our ego talking. Keep an open mind regarding your pay and the benefits that you receive. In time, your good performance will be rewarded with the compensation that you believe you deserve.

Early in my career, after obtaining my Masters degree, I decided to leave the field of education to enter the business world. I had a specific salary in mind that I wanted to earn. The offer that I received was lower than I had anticipated, and certainly lower than I desired. At first, I was inclined to reject the offer.

The man who offered the job to me suggested that I look at the difference in what I wanted and what I was offered as the price that I would have to pay for the opportunity to gain experience in the industry. He reasoned that I had just paid to get my Masters degree in a field that would help me enter private enterprise. Since the only experience I had in this field was during summers in college, he believed that he was offering me a fair salary for the chance to prove that I could do the job. I took the job. A new position opened up within the company six months later that gave me an opportunity to combine what I had learned on the new job with my teaching experience. I was promoted into that new job, and wound up making more in the first year with the company than I had anticipated when I interviewed for the first job.

When you demonstrate your receptivity to new ideas and ways of doing things, people are more likely to listen to your ideas seriously. Adapting to change and developing a flexible attitude gets easier over time. Each success that you acquire from doing something new and different will increase your self-esteem and confidence that you can do it again and again.

When you adapt to a change and don't like the results that you get, ask yourself what you learned from the situation. Then ask yourself how you CAN flex your attitude to accommodate and accept the results rather than making yourself miserable by focusing on what you CAN'T do because of the change.

You see that office politics sometimes creates conditions that you won't like. Rather than stew about it, adapt to conditions as you find them, and figure out what you *can* do to see the conditions in a different light. One way to do this is to ask your network for ideas on how they've adapted to changing situations successfully. Learning to be flexible and adapt to changes will reduce much of the stress and frustration in the workplace and life that affect your success.

TIPS to S O A R [Seize Opportunities And Rewards]

❖ You will work with some people whom you won't particularly care for. You will, however, be expected to work with these people effectively, as a united team.

❖ Knowing the right people can often help you get what you want or accomplish what you need to do.

❖ The cardinal rule in dealing with office politics is to be aware of them and keep your wits about you. Do the job that you were hired to do in the best manner that you possibly can.

❖ Regardless of whom you know, you'll need to earn an endorsement, appointment, or promotion based on your own merit and worthiness for the appointment.

❖ Networking is your conscious effort to meet people with whom you can share information to help each other achieve goals and objectives. It occurs in your professional and personal life.

❖ We find, in the workplace and life, that we have to try new methods and accept others' suggestions to truly get what we want.

What tips from chapter 10 do *you* value most?
List them here:

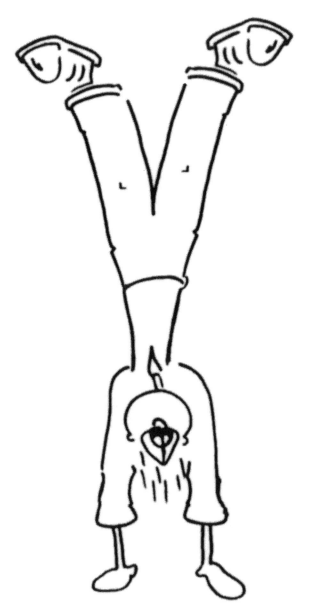

You want flexible? I'll show you flexible ☺

- Chapter 11 -

And you thought No One Noticed

W ho do you know that can ...?

"Who you are speaks so loud, I can't hear the words you are saying" - Ralph Waldo Emerson

Much of your success in the workplace and life depends on the type of person that you are and how you present yourself.

Successful people take care of themselves and reap associated rewards for their efforts in the workplace and life. They know their strengths and abilities, stay in good physical shape, dress appropriately for different occasions, walk and talk confidently and speak courteously. They do this not so much to impress others, but to reinforce for themselves that they're worth the effort. When you believe in yourself, others will believe in you also.

People are drawn to those who care about themselves and express this care effectively. You can demonstrate your self-care in the workplace and life through your image, communication, and continuous learning.

Image

Your image is the picture that you hold of yourself in your mind and what you show to others. It is reflected in how you look, dress, speak and move. You show that you believe in yourself when you are well groomed, dress neatly and speak courteously and clearly.

You can do this regardless of your socio-economic status, educational background, or environment. The choice is yours! What do you believe about yourself and want others to see?

Grooming, hygiene, clothing, and body language all send messages to the world about how you feel about yourself. This includes your hairstyle, the fragrances you wear, your teeth, posture, and vocabulary. A few basic pieces of clothing that are appropriate to your workplace and activities are sufficient. Keep them clean, well pressed and in good condition.

You only get one chance to make a good first impression! To increase your chances of succeeding in the workplace and life, invest the time and energy to take care of yourself.

You will attract the kind of people that have similar values and beliefs as you do. Likewise, you will find employment with the type of company that believes you will represent it *properly*. Properly means in a manner that appeals to and attracts customers.

How you look, dress, and speak tells the world what you think about yourself. Expressing your individuality is fine, as long as you respect others' right to do the same. If you disregard the company's dress code and preferred image, you may have difficulty building credibility. In some cases, blatant disregard for company practices will stifle your growth potential.

Each business and industry defines its preferred image for its employees. This includes dress code and standards of grooming.

Big and medium-sized businesses, referred to as 'Corporate America', require male employees to wear suits and ties or sports jackets at work - both in the office and while traveling. Many companies used to, and some still do, prefer that their senior executives have no facial hair, wear only minimal conservative jewelry, and laced shoes. The rule about facial hair is relaxing, as long as employees look professional, neat and clean.

Female employees are expected to wear suits or dresses, or skirts, blouses and jackets to work. They are expected to wear hosiery and closed toed shoes of moderate height heels. This is as much for the employees' safety as it is for company image. You're safer with moderate to conservative versus flamboyant clothing. Provocative clothing and demeanor is unacceptable. Throughout the 1990s, pantsuits became popular for women and they became more acceptable in business.

Dress code has been a focal point in the workplace for the past decade. A company's dress code is designed to reflect the company's image, show respect to its customers and that employees care about themselves. This care is reflected in the quality of their work.

How do you feel when you're wearing a suit and tie or special outfit? Wearing blue jeans and tee shirts signals to your mind that you're playing, not working. Business offices that have an established dress code distinguish three categories - business attire, business casual, and dress down.

Business attire refers to the normal everyday clothing that employees are expected to wear. At all times, this should be professional, neat and clean and is the formal type of dress described above.

Business casual is more relaxed clothing often referred to as sports clothing. For men this means shirt, slax, and sports coat or sweater but no tie. For women, this means more casual blouses and skirts or slax, but not denim.

Dress down refers to the most relaxed type of clothing acceptable in the work environment. This includes blue jeans or denim skirts, tee shirts, and sneakers, as long as they are clean and in good condition.

Many businesses that operate in offices reward employees by allowing them to dress casually on certain days during the week, and dress down on Fridays. Business offices in the computer industry and some smaller companies often allow their employees to dress business casual all the time. Likewise, some employees in the retail industry dress less formally than those who work in an office. While it is totally acceptable to dress like employees in big business, it's not expected.

Other industries accept and expect employees to dress according to their job and working conditions. Auto mechanics that work in a garage wear overalls and work boots. Food service employees must wear aprons and hairnets when preparing and serving food. Hospital workers and laboratory employees wear lab coats or aprons. Entertainers wear more flamboyant clothing to dazzle the public.

Several industries and professions have a specific uniform. You can always spot a police officer, fireman, or postal worker by their uniform. An employee wearing that uniform thinks of him or herself accordingly and performs the type and quality of service expected from the role that he or she is filling.

Regarding your image, clothing is like the gift wrapping on a present. The prettier the package, the nicer you expect the present inside to be. With clothing and grooming, the more attractive the package, the more confident and competent the person is expected to be.

If you go through life thinking, "Why bother? Who will notice or care?" you will reflect this in your dress and hygiene. You may appear sloppy, wear worn out clothing, slouch and/or frown when you meet people.

In truth, people do notice, even if they don't say anything about it. And more people care than you may realize. Most importantly, you do matter and would be wise to care about yourself. The effort that you put into grooming your mind, body, and abilities pays tangible and intangible rewards in every aspect of your life. Putting your best foot forward increases your chances of obtaining the job(s) that you want and helps you build relationships with others whom you want and need in your life.

Getting those jobs will usually involve interviewing with one or more people in an organization. Always assume that a company follows business dress code and dress accordingly for the interview. Once an employee, you will learn when it's acceptable to dress differently, and what items of clothing are acceptable.

Interviews

Interviews are your opportunity to show the company why you would be a good addition to their team. Your interview [telephone or in person] will be your first exposure to the company. The first thing that an interviewer notices about you is your image - how you look and carry yourself [in person] or how confidently you speak [on the telephone]. He or she will form an impression about you within the first 10 seconds of meeting or talking to you.

You only get one chance to make a good first impression!

When you meet someone new, and especially when you go to an interview, stand tall, hold your head high, SMILE ☺, and extend your hand for a welcome handshake. [Firmly clasp their hand in yours without crushing it, and shake it *three* times. Crushing someone's hand indicates that you are aggressive. Merely putting out your hand like a limp rag implies that you lack self-confidence or are overly timid.]

Be well groomed and dress appropriately for an interview. This means a clean shirt, tie and suit or jacket for men and a clean blouse, skirt and jacket or suit or dress for women. Even if you are interviewing for a position in the warehouse, where the dress code more likely is dress down, you increase your chances of getting the job when you come to the interview dressed in business attire.

Candidates, who have an idea of what they like, perform better on interviews than those who stare blankly at the interviewer without any ideas. Tell the interviewer(s) about your skills and interests. Then tell him or her what your strengths are by sharing examples of successes in school, sports, team projects, etc. You can ask him or her what jobs are available for someone with your skills and interests. You and the interviewer may make a decision together as to which job would be the best for you to consider.

Arrive for your interview a few minutes early. Most companies will ask you to complete an employment application, which could take some time. If you're going to be late for an interview, call the interviewer to let him or her know. Business people schedule many activities during their day and your being late for an appointment could interfere with the interviewer's busy schedule. If you don't call to explain that you may be late, he or she may perceive that you are irresponsible and lackadaisical, which could negatively affect your chances of getting the job.

Be courteous to the receptionist who greets you. Clearly state your name and whom you are there to see. While completing your application, and while you are waiting for the interviewer to greet you, note the surroundings and employees' attitudes. Smile at the employees and listen to how they communicate with each other.

When you interview for a job, you will most likely meet someone in the Human Resources department of the company first, or the business owner if it is a small business. If the first interview goes well, you may be invited to meet other people, including the person you would work for called 'the hiring manager'. You may also meet some of your colleagues or team members.

Interviewers will evaluate your response to their questions to determine three criteria – *can* do, *will* do, and *fit*. 'Can-do' refers to your technical ability to perform the essential functions of the role.

If you have completed the education and demonstrated specific technical skills required to perform the job, the interviewer will determine that you *can do* the job that is required. Usually the hiring manager determines your technical competence and whether you 'can do' the job.

'Will-do' refers to your attitude about work, yourself, and others. An optimistic, positive attitude usually implies that you will do whatever is necessary to get the job done without undue complaining. How you feel about working with other people also indicates how well you will perform as a team member, and contribute to the company's overall objectives.

Human Resources interviewers and peers/colleagues often determine your attitude and whether you *'will do'* the job, if hired. Your willingness to take on new challenges and responsibilities and stay focused on these objectives indicates your leadership skills. Leadership is needed at all levels of an organization. Employees at any level can demonstrate leadership, not just management.

Your appearance and image are the first signs of how well you *'fit'* into an organization. This is revealed in how you look, dress, speak, and carry yourself. The Human Resources interviewer will determine this. If he or she believes that you don't 'fit', it is unlikely that you will get to see the other interviewers.

All interviewers will assess your judgement and reasoning skills, your motivation to work, your competencies [knowledge, skills and abilities], what value you would add to their organization, your self-concept [confidence without being cocky or arrogant], your attitude, personality and what kind of team player you would be on their staff.

Be sure to answer the question that was asked. If you are unsure about what was asked, ask the interviewer to repeat the question. Most interviewers will want to cover these basics and may ask the following questions:

COMMON INTERVIEW QUESTIONS

1. What kind of work do you want to do? Why?

[This question will determine if you know your strengths and developmental opportunities]

2. Which teachers or supervisors have you found easiest to work with and which have been most difficult?
    [Your answer to this question determines your adaptability.]

3. When have you had to get a point across to different types of people? Tell me what you said and did.
    [This explores your communication skills.]

4. Describe a school or work-related problem that you faced recently. What was the problem and what did you do to resolve it? [This explores your problem solving and decision-making skills]

5. Give me an example of a time when you did something or accomplished more than you were required or expected to do. [This tests your initiative.]

6. Give me an example of a time when you found it necessary to make an exception to the rules in order to get something done. [This question will assess your integrity]

7. Tell me about your experience as a team member.
    [This question evaluates your ability to work in a team.]

8. Tell me about a time when you had to influence others to produce a certain result. What did you do? How effective were you? [This question will assess your Leadership.]

9. Have you ever had trouble learning a new subject, method or procedure? What was it and how did you deal with that situation? [This is investigating your learning ability.]

10. Based on all the candidates that I have to interview, why should we hire you for this position? [This question assesses your self-confidence, and makes sure that you give consistent answers during your interview.]

If you have prior work experience, you may also hear the following questions:

1. What have you been doing since your last position?

2. What did you most like/dislike about each of your past positions?

3. Why did you leave your last position?

4. What are your strengths, specifically?

5. What are your weaknesses?

Different interviewers ask these questions in various ways. At the very least, the interviewer wants to know:

❖ Why you're looking for a new job
❖ What experience you have
❖ What kind of work you're best suited to
❖ What value you can add to their organization
❖ What kind of team player you will be, and
❖ Why should they hire you?

In addition, you will also be asked, what questions do you have? It is a good idea to do some research about the company and ask some questions to show that you're interested in the company and not just looking for a job. Do NOT ask about the salary and benefits that you will receive. You can discuss this after an offer is made.

When you anticipate the interviewer's questions and practice your answers in advance, you will perform better during the interview. Giving good answers to the interviewer's questions is no guarantee that you will get the job for which you are interviewing.

You must convince the interviewer that you can truly do everything that you said you could do. To do this, make each of your answers a S T A R. Listen carefully to the question and then respond by telling the interviewer:
The specific Situation or Task that you faced, the Action that you took, and the Result that your actions produced.

For example, when asked about your experience as a team member, rather than simply say, "I worked on a group project at school" you will want to explain: " I led the team project for my Humanities class. We were asked to complete a community service project.

I organized and led a group of five students that sponsored a needy family at Christmastime. We made a list of each family member's name, age, and sex, and decided what kind of gifts to buy for each. Then we held a bake sale and auction, and sold candy to raise money for the family. After buying gifts for each person, we prepared a festive dinner and, together, brought everything to the family's home in time for Christmas."

How would *you* answer the questions listed above?

 Terri Levine, Coach at Comprehensive Coaching in North Wales, Pennsylvania suggests that "You may want to say your answers out loud while looking in a mirror to see how you look and sound." She also suggests that you record your answers into a tape recorder and play them back to see how you sound. Her final suggestion is, "...after practicing your answers, take charge of your career to get the job that you want and find the employer that you want to work for! "

During the interview, demonstrate to the interviewer(s) that you are most interested in the position and what you can do to help the company serve its customers. If you are the chosen candidate, the company will offer you a fair salary and benefits, based on competitive jobs within the same field and geographical area.

Your answers to the interview questions will determine your ability to do the job, and reveal your values. Research into successful careers shows that employees work best for companies whose values are similar to the employee's own.

Regardless of the outcome, look at every interview as a learning experience. The people you meet, the questions they ask, and your response to those questions all present opportunities for you to learn more about yourself and different work environments.

Learning doesn't end when you graduate from school. Your graduation is merely the beginning of your life as an adult. That's why graduation is called *commencement* and not completion ☺

Lifelong Learning

"The great breakthrough in your life comes when you realize that you can learn anything you need to learn to achieve any goal you set for yourself"- Brian Tracy

The one thing that you can count on in the workplace and life is continuous change. New technology and the increased capacity to communicate globally bring new ideas, methods, products and services to the workplace and society on a regular basis.

In order for some companies to remain leaders in their industry and markets during continuous change, they merge with competitors and/or acquire smaller companies that produce the same product or services. When a company merges with or acquires another, employees from the prior individual companies become employees of one new and larger company. Oftentimes, this results in too many employees performing similar jobs. One way that some companies minimize their expenses and maximize profits is to eliminate positions and terminate the employment of employees. We talked about this process called 'Downsizing' in chapter 2.

The first thing that you need to know about 'Downsizing' is that it's purely a business decision.. Too many employees take downsizing personally and interpret the company's actions as a personal affront to the individual employee. When a company's management decides to eliminate positions and terminate employees' employment, it's to save the money that it costs to pay employees' salary, benefits, and taxes. Reducing expenses increases profits and allows the company to continue.

Management determines which employees' jobs will be eliminated. When a job is eliminated, all employees who perform that job are evaluated. Those who lose their jobs do so based on their performance and value to the organization. Employees who have most contributed to the company's growth and continuously improve their competence [knowledge, skills, and abilities] are the last ones to lose their jobs, if at all. In many instances, an employee whose position has been eliminated may be asked to assume a different role in the organization because of the value that he or she has demonstrated through their performance.

In order to sustain *your* employability, demonstrate the ability to keep up with the pace of change, remain flexible and adaptable. This often requires that you learn new skills and operating procedures. Successful people make continuous learning a life-long habit. They read books in their own field to develop the expertise that makes them attractive to companies who need that particular skill or talent.

Employable people read books in other fields to develop new skills and expand their opportunities for employment. People who succeed in the workplace and life also listen to audiotape programs, watch videos, and attend classes, seminars, and workshops to expand their knowledge. This also expands their network of potential contacts for future employment opportunities.

Employers' biggest complaint today is the lack of qualified candidates to fill the open positions. In 1998, 347,000 jobs in computer technology were unfilled. If you open the Employment Classified section of any newspaper, you will see scores of jobs that are available on a regular basis.

In his book, <u>The Fifth Discipline</u>, Peter Senge tells employers that their most sustainable competitive advantage is a work force of competent employees. During a nationwide teleconference on January 12, 1999, Vice President Al Gore told business leaders and educators that an employee's most valuable traits would be continuous learning and the ability to improve their contribution to their employers.

Your continuously learning about yourself, the workplace and life, will be reflected in your image, how you communicate and conduct yourself on interviews and involvement with others. You won't have to tell other people that you're a continuous learner. Your new knowledge and skills will be revealed in your appropriate behavior, self-confidence and performance in the workplace and life.

TIPS TO SOAR [Seize Opportunities And Rewards]

❖ Much of your success in the workplace and life depends on the type of person that you are and how you present yourself.

❖ You show that you believe in yourself when you are well groomed, dress attractively and speak courteously and clearly.

❖ Interviewers will evaluate your response to their questions to determine three criteria – *can* do, *will* do, and *fit*. 'Can-do' refers to your technical ability to perform the essential functions of the role.

❖ Make each of your answers to interview questions a **S T A R**. Listen carefully to the question and then respond by telling the interviewer the specific **S**ituation or **T**ask that you faced, the **A**ction that you took, and the **R**esult that your actions produced.

❖ During the interview, demonstrate to the interviewer(s) that you are most interested in the position and what you can do to help the company serve its customers.

❖ Your continuous learning about yourself, the workplace and life, will be reflected in your image, how you communicate and conduct yourself on interviews and involvement with others.

What tips from chapter 11 do *you* value most?
List them below:

What Job are you applying for?

- Chapter 12 -

If it's to be, it's up to me!

I've spread my wings. Watch me S O A R!

"You miss 100% of the shots you never take."
- Wayne Gretsky

The work place and life areas exciting or ominous, as you want or allow them to be. The ABCs to your success in the workplace and in life are *YOUR*:

* ❖ <u>A</u>ttitude
* ❖ <u>B</u>eliefs, and
* ❖ <u>C</u>ommitment.

Your **attitude** determines how you perceive things and the actions that you take to progress, succeed and grow.
Your **beliefs** determine how you process and incorporate the advice, feedback and information that you give yourself and receive from others.
Your **commitment** determines the effort that you put towards achieving your goals and fulfilling your purpose in life.

ATTITUDE

When you're interviewing for a job, your attitude will be a major factor in whether you are selected. During my career in Human Resources, the interview team always discussed a candidate's attitude when determining how well we thought that he or she would perform on the job and fit into the organization. Interviewers decide whom to hire for a position based on candidates' attitude, competencies (knowledge, skills, and abilities), and relevant experience, if required.

239

My experience shows that candidates with positive attitudes are more willing to do whatever is required to perform their job. They are more dependable and show up for work regularly, despite problems with weather or other inconveniences. Their attitude helps them focus, which results in effective performance and creates positive morale in the company.

Candidates with negative attitudes usually see the worst in any situation. They whine and complain about the things that they don't like, performing poorly and creating low morale among their colleagues.

I used to advertise open positions and often received hundreds of resumes and applications. From these, I selected initial candidates to call based on their qualifications - education, experience, and written communication skills. During the telephone screening [first stage in the interviewing process], I asked questions to confirm their qualifications.

How a candidate answered my questions indicated their motivation to work and their attitude. Many times I spoke to more than 50 candidates to find just 5 that I would invite to interview in person.

I've seen jobs remain vacant for as long as 10 months because the applicants who apply lack either the skills or attitude necessary to perform well. To increase *your* success in the workplace and life, develop a positive "I can!" attitude. A positive attitude gives you the courage to try new things, the willingness to support your team in achieving business objectives, and helps you smile during adverse conditions. This makes you more pleasant to be around, and helps you build gratifying relationships, professionally and personally.

240

Wake up every morning with the thought, "If it's to be, it's up to me!"

Approach each activity, event, and challenge knowing that you *can* make a difference. You will accomplish what you set out to, as long as you are clear on your objective, assess current conditions for what they are and *think* about what actions and words will help you accomplish your desired outcome.

Sometimes, when you face a difficult challenge, you may not even try to do the task. Instead of talking yourself *out* of a situation, talk yourself *in* to it. Use the acronym **MOOMBA– My Only Obstacle Must Be My Attitude** – to convince yourself that it's worth the effort. You'll find that when you adopt a positive attitude, you will believe in your abilities more and succeed.

Successful people recognize that failures are what make us succeed in the future. By learning from your mistakes or failed efforts, you'll know how to approach the situation differently to produce better results. Maintaining this attitude drives the beliefs that keep you going.

Michael Jordan, the NBA Champion, was quoted as saying "I've missed more than 9000 shots in my career, lost almost 300 games. Twenty six times I've been trusted to take the winning game shot and missed. I've failed over and over and over again in my life. And *that* is why I succeed. If you're not failing from time to time, you are not pushing yourself, and if you are not pushing yourself, your life is destined to be a sorry litany of mightas and couldas."

Besides your own attitude, how do other people's attitudes affect you? Are you attracted to people with positive attitudes and resist or avoid people who have lousy attitudes? Why do you do this? We gravitate towards people with positive attitudes because we feel better being around them. We tend to avoid negative people because their attitude drains our energy; they're no fun to be around.

If you don't believe this, try this little experiment. First, even if you don't feel like it, smile and say out loud, I feel great! [Oh, come on! Try it. Notice how you feel.] Then, frown and say, I'm miserable. [Now how do you feel?] When you see that your attitude can change how you actually feel, doesn't it make sense to choose feeling great over feeling miserable?

Your attitude shapes your BELIEFS. A positive attitude and associated beliefs allow you to take risks to learn new skills and learn from your mistakes instead of giving up. How is *your* attitude helping or holding you back from getting the job or building the relationships that you desire?

BELIEFS

"Be not afraid of life. Believe that life is worth living, and your belief will help create the fact" William James

There is a difference between just saying that you believe something and really believing it. How can you know the difference? When you truly believe in yourself and your abilities, you will welcome opportunities and conquer your fears. After all, in most cases fear is nothing more than **F**alse **E**vidence **A**ppearing **R**eal. Many times if you do what you've been afraid of, you realize that the situation turned out better than you expected.

242

Suppose you let fear of rejection prevent you from applying for a job that you really want or asking someone you like to go out with you. When you complete the application and get the job, or ask the person out and are accepted, you realize that it was much easier than you thought and you enjoyed the process.

One way to overcome this fear is to ask yourself, "What's the worst that could happen?" The answer is usually that someone will tell you "no". If someone says no, you're in the *same* condition that you were before your asked, no better and no worse. However, based on the law of probability, there's an equal or better chance that they may say "Yes". Then you're better off than you were before you asked.

When I started my business, I was reluctant to ask other training professionals to use my services. Once I convinced myself that I was offering something that other people need, use and want, I developed more business than I had anticipated. Now that I'm serving many satisfied clients, people come to me for my services without my having to ask.

When you believe in yourself and your abilities, you will apply for jobs that interest you, and in which *you* believe you can perform well. It won't matter whether others believe that you can do the job.
Belief gives you the motivation to test your skills and experience success.
Believing in yourself also gives you the courage to approach someone new, without fearing that they may not like you. This will help you network with others as we discussed in chapter 10. People who believe in themselves are able to take rejection without damaging their beliefs.

Believing in yourself means that you know your strengths and limitations, without allowing them to destroy your confidence. You take *calculated* risks, knowing that you will succeed in your efforts. A calculated risk is one that you think about carefully and recognize that you have nothing to lose by simply going for it. If the risk you're about to take has a greater probability to result in harm for you or others, then your fear is justified and you you'd be wise to refuse it. Believing in yourself does not mean being foolhardy about the risks that you take.

For example, suppose someone asked you to walk across a beam that is 8 inches wide and 50-feet long without falling off. To make it worth your while, they'll give you a prize when you reach the other end. Would you do this? You would if the prize is something you want and you believe that you could do it. You'd hop right onto the beam and start walking.

However, suppose that the beam was suspended 2,000 feet up in the air between two skyscrapers. Would you still hop on to the beam and cross it for the prize? ONLY if you thought that the prize was worth it AND you truly believed that you could do it, safely.

Considering the variables just introduced, your mind would probably question whether you could make it safely across. The questions generate appropriate fear and you'd probably refuse the challenge. In life, *Whether you think you can, or you think you can't, you're right.* So, choose to think that you can!

Remember the storybook from grade school about the little engine that could? A small train faced a steep uphill climb that others thought impossible for him to achieve.

244

The little engine refused to listen to other's doubts about his ability. Through determination, and constantly telling himself, "I think I can, I think I can" he reached the top.

The engine's attitude made him *believe* that he could make it to the top. Had the engine failed to make it to the top of the hill, his positive attitude and belief system would have made him examine the reasons why he failed. Then he could gather his strength and begin again.

The same holds true with our beliefs in the workplace and life situations. When we are convinced that we can accomplish what we are asked to do, we jump right in. When we don't fully believe that we can do something that we are asked to do, we often hesitate or resist.

Chances are you'll never be asked to cross the beam at 1,000 feet in the air. Never the less, your beliefs about what you *can* accomplish influence what you choose to do and how well you will perform in the workplace and life.

Today's workplace is constantly changing. We are told that successful people are those who adopt a habit of life-long learning. Our beliefs give us the courage to persist despite adversity. If you have successfully learned new things in the past, and people told you how smart you are, you probably believe that you are smart, and capable of learning new things.

This belief helps you tackle a new subject, confident that you will learn it. If you've had difficulty in school, people called you 'dummy' or told you that you're stupid, you probably believe that you can't learn anything new. This belief will hold you back and prevent you from getting what you want out of life.

It's important to recognize that other people's *opinions* of you do not determine what you are capable of. When he was in high school, movie producer Steven Speilberg was told that he would never amount to anything. What do you think the people who told him that are saying now? They're probably bragging about the fact that they knew Steven when he was a boy.

When he was in grade school, teachers told Leslie (Les) Calvin Brown, now a professional speaker, that he was educably retarded. He let this belief prevent him from asserting himself. Fortunately, one high school teacher told Les that other people's *opinions* do not determine who he is. This teacher inspired Les to develop the self-confidence to create a new belief system.

Les became a professional speaker, author, television and radio host who speaks to people about believing in themselves. He is very successful, commanding $20,000 or more an hour to speak to various audiences.

Oher people's comments may cause you to question yourself. Their comments should make you question their judgements. After all, opinions are not facts, they're judgements. Your self-perception and beliefs determine what you are truly capable of achieving.

I worked for a man, who said to me regularly, " What a bizarre woman you are!" The first time he said it, I thought he was teasing me, so I shrugged it off. [We need to be able to laugh at ourselves]. When it became a regular issue, I found that I let his comments make me doubt my abilities. I didn't like how I was feeling, and asked him to stop.

Upon realizing that we just think differently [see chapter 8 on behavioral styles], I stopped allowing his comments to affect me. That didn't make either one of us right or wrong, good or bad, just different. Once I *accepted* the fact that our minds operate differently, I stopped paying attention to his remarks. Then I examined my own beliefs about what I can do well and pursued opportunities to practice those skills with others that appreciate them.

I am now doing things that I believe I do well and enjoy! My rewards come from the thanks I get from people who believe that I've helped them discover their own value, abilities and self-esteem. Remind yourself that you can accomplish anything that you set your mind to.

" Our deepest fear is not that we are inadequate. Our deepest fear is that we are powerful beyond measure. It is our light, not our darkness that most frightens us. We ask ourselves, Who am I to be brilliant, gorgeous, talented, fabulous? Actually, who are you not to be? Your playing small doesn't serve the world. There's nothing enlightened about shrinking so that other people won't feel insecure around you. You are born to make manifest the glory of God that is within you. It's not just in some of us, it's in everyone. And as we let our own light shine, we unconsciously give other people permission to do the same. We're liberated from our own fear, our presence automatically liberates others." -
Attributed to Nelson Mandella

Your beliefs about your abilities give you confidence. Confidence makes it easy for you to commit yourself to the things and people that matter most to you.

COMMITMENT

To commit is to entrust or promise something to someone or some entity. When you make a commitment to yourself or someone else, it means that you will deliver some service or support. Living up to your commitments builds integrity and character. When you commit yourself to doing a specific task or deed, or providing a service, you are telling the recipient that they can count on you to do what you said you would do.

You show your commitment at work by consistently showing up each day, doing your job, and producing quality work despite other conditions or circumstances in your life. For example, when you were in school, if it snowed, school would close and you didn't have to show up. Businesses don't close for snow, unless it is so severe that the state declares an emergency and the roads are impassable.

You show commitment to your relationships when you agree to do something for a family member, friend, co-worker, significant other, etc. and then do or deliver what you promised. If you agree to complete a project by a specific date, your commitment will show by the effort that you exert to meet that deadline and deliver a quality project.

Sometimes you depend on others to provide information or complete part of the project with you. When you are committed, even if others fail to do their part, you will find the appropriate way to communicate your needs and do what is necessary to complete the project. OR, well before the deadline, you will tell the people expecting the finished project that you're unable to deliver it as promised, and for what reasons.

While they may not like it, people will understand that you can't always meet deadlines as long as you're honest and tell them far enough in advance for them to adjust their expectations. If you resist telling someone the truth because you don't want to disappoint him or her, you'll disappoint them more by withholding information.

When you are committed to a relationship, professional or personal, you will continue to support the other person regardless of any differences that may exist in your values or beliefs. For example, suppose that one of your colleagues is having difficulty performing their job. Instead of ignoring this person and treating him or her with disgust, you can help them figure out how to improve their performance by asking them questions to stimulate their thinking.

Then you can educate them about the resources available to help them learn their job. Supporting and being committed to a relationship does NOT mean that you do everything for the other person. It means that you express your concern and remain open to listening to them whenever they need a friend. The best way that you can help others is to coach them into doing things for themselves.

You demonstrate your commitment to *yourself* by staying true to your beliefs and values. If someone asks you to do something that you don't agree with, commit to staying true to your beliefs by tactfully refusing to do what you are asked. For example, suppose you work for a retail store and have access to the supply room. If one of your friends asked you to steal some supplies because 'no one will ever notice', and you value honesty, you will tell your friend that you are not willing to do that. Then you might find out why they want the product(s)

249

and offer to help him or her think of ways to raise the money to buy them outright.

You will find yourself succeeding in the workplace and life when you consistently apply these ABCs. Your attitude, beliefs, and commitment show through in every action and interaction you perform. Your attitude, beliefs, and commitment will be evident to others in the way that you develop and apply each skill covered in this book.

These include how you:

❖ Choose your direction
❖ Understand business
❖ Think and solve problems,
❖ Plan and organize your work,
❖ Adapt to changing conditions,
❖ Accept responsibility and maintain accountability for your actions,
❖ Communicate [verbally, non-verbally and in writing],
❖ Demonstrate leadership
❖ Design your image
❖ Treat others inter-personally.

Every work place and life experience is an opportunity to learn. Consider learning a life-long process. It doesn't stop when you complete your schooling. And schooling doesn't end when you've earned your degree(s). As a human being, you are constantly growing, capable of learning and seizing opportunities to apply what you learn.

CONTINUOUS LEARNING

Adults learn best when they are motivated to do so.

Research into the adult learning process reveals that adults learn best when using training programs that offer:
1. *Variety* in content and delivery
2. *Relevance* to their specific needs
3. *Interaction* with others
4. *Autonomy* in how to apply information on the job and in their life
5. *Reinforcement of* other knowledge

Motivation is often part of one's personal *strategy* that you want to achieve. Your strategy is like your business plan or road map in life. It tells you where you are headed, what you want to achieve and how you plan to achieve it. You achieve your strategy by executing your plan, which is the process that lists the tactics you will follow to achieve your strategy.

Tom Leonard, founder of Coach University, says that succeeding in the workplace and life today depends on having the *right* strategy. The right strategy ensures a successful outcome. The *wrong* strategy is one that is no longer useful or wastes valuable resources and needlessly delays results. The trick to selecting your perfect strategy is to create it from scratch. The following information about strategies is adapted from Tom Leonard's "Top Ten Ways to Create a Strategy for Influence" © 1999

In the old days, you succeeded through hard work, commitment, effort, dedication and "following the rules". It worked, and in some cases still does, but was often too costly, physically, emotionally, and spiritually. Smart people are no longer willing to *suffer* for success.

Strategizing is a skill; one that you can benefit from forever in your career, business and personal life. The integral parts of executing your strategy are your:

VISION: What's possible. A vision is what you see that others may not see. It's about improvement, betterment, sheer possibility, yet it's not pie-in-the-sky (that's called a pipe dream).

PURPOSE: The goal that you want to achieve to fulfill your vision and why you are doing what you are doing.

OUTCOMES: What happens after you reach your objective or goal. The outcome includes the results and the benefits of those results, both tangible and intangible.

STRATEGY: Your approach, or positioning. It's your smart way of reaching the goal with the least amount of wasted effort or cost.

PLAN: How you organize and schedule your time, resources and energy. A plan is the process of executing your strategy. It consists of a list of resources needed, action steps to take, and a timeline of events and milestones to measure your progress.

Sometimes with a strategy, you're working on conditions that affect the goal rather than the goal itself. These include improving the environment, relationships, resources, systems or even you. Strategies are different from the plan. The right strategy drives the plan. The plan often becomes obvious. Without the strategy, the plan is merely a set of action steps with no specific outcome or purpose.

The right strategy helps you maximize your resources while expanding the goal and outcomes.

A strategy can be as simple as a play in the football game, or as complex as building a new e-business. Create *your* strategy by asking yourself some questions:

1. What's the smartest, most creative and easiest way to make X happen, without doing it like everyone else is trying to do it?
2. What's a better way?
3. What's an unconventional way?
4. What's MY way?"

You may choose to draft your strategy alone, or with help from others. Either way, be true to your own purpose. Let the following poem guide you as you face the challenges of building your success. Though written in the masculine gender, it is equally applicable to females:

CHARGE, author unknown

If you think you are beaten, you are
If you think you dare not, you don't
If you'd like to win but think you can't
It's almost certain you won't.
If you think you'll lose, you've lost
For out in the world you'll find,
Success begins with a fellow's will
It's all in a state of mind.
If you think you're outclassed, you are
You've got to think high to rise
You've got to be sure of yourself
Before you can win a prize.

Life's battles don't always go to the stronger or faster man
But sooner or later the man who wins is
The man who thinks he can!

New situations and environments can be confusing. Learn
from others who have succeeded in what you want to do.
When you face a new situation or environment, spend time
observing how others perform. Ask questions, and think about
your behavior before acting. Operating purely on instinct may
result in actions that are inappropriate for that environment.
Choose behaviors that are most appropriate for the setting and
circumstances.

Life is full of choices. Each choice has a consequence. When
you choose behavior or actions that are appropriate for your
role, business, and relationships you are more likely to receive
praise and recognition for doing a good job without having to
ask for it.

Choose behavior that is appropriate for your role, the business,
teams, or relationships. This will strengthen them and make
them last. James Treybig, president of Tandem Computers
said: "There are three types of people in this world:

Those who make things happen
Those who watch what happens, and
Those how ask, What happened?"

Which type are you now and which will you commit to be from
now on?

Many people will give you advice as you build your career and
life. You may choose to listen to or ignore the advice and

feedback you receive. If you trust the person who's giving it, and choose to follow the advice you receive, you will most likely learn something about yourself that you can develop into a new skill.

Learning increases self-confidence and esteem. Self-confidence and esteem result in your choosing appropriate behaviors in the future. If you choose to ignore the feedback that you receive from others and continue to behave inappropriately for the environment, be prepared for the consequences. Likewise, if you behave inappropriately in your personal relationships, you may lose support of people whom you want in your life. When you lack confidence in your skills and abilities to perform what a job requires, act 'as if' you do possess these skills.

The term 'act' here means to behave in a manner that is appropriate for the situation, not to try to pull the wool over someone's eyes or get away with something. By 'acting as-if', you convince yourself that this is natural behavior for you. The mind cannot distinguish between that which is vividly imagined and that which is real.

The longer and more convincingly you 'act as if', the sooner you will learn the behavior appropriate to your role. What you focus on intensifies. Thinking about the appropriate way to perform the job will make you repeat it often, as it will become your strength. What you resist persists, and if you focus on what you lack, you'll continue to be ill prepared for your job.

Be honest with yourself and your supervisor about areas where you need help and want to develop skill. After you receive guidance, practice the new method or technique to develop the skills you need to succeed.

Watch and learn from those around you who are proficient in their performance. In addition, read everything you can about a particular subject that will help you gain knowledge that you can turn into skill. Competence in a job is having the knowledge, skills, and ability to perform that job effectively. Knowledge comes from information. Depending on your preferred learning style, you can gather this information from books, audiotapes, videos, lectures, interactive exercises in workshops, observing others, and doing the actual work (on-the-job training).

Skills are talents that you develop from practicing and applying knowledge to a particular situation. When practiced repeatedly, you won't have to think as hard about doing it again. Recognize, however, that each situation is unique. You will still need to think about which behavior is appropriate for *that* occasion. By developing different skills and abilities, you'll have more choices to apply in different situations.

Ability is the attitude, desire, and physical capability to perform a certain task. You are the master of your own fate. Select the career path that interests you. Muster all your courage, believe that you can achieve what you set your mind to, and you will. Some jobs will include activities or tasks that you don't enjoy. Adopting a 'can-do' attitude will keep you focused on achieving your goal even when you don't enjoy doing some of the things you have to do to get there.

Brian Tracy, international speaker, is just one of the people who tells us that the only security in life is to count on your own abilities and efforts. Rather than expect life-long employment, it is wiser to believe in life-long employability. This means that, whether in reality or imagined, you are the president of your own company. Consider that you lease yourself to employers as if they're your clients or customers.

Earl Nightingale is often quoted for explaining the secret to success as this: "You become what you think about. What your mind can conceive and believe, you can achieve!" Being clear about your interests and what motivates you determines what you want to do.

Thinking about this helps you discover the right way to achieve what you want, and the resources you need will become available. Picture yourself achieving what you want to and you will make it happen!

List the things that you want here:

❖ _____

❖ _____

❖ _____

❖ _____

❖ _____

❖ _____

❖ _____

To get what you want, target the type of work that you'd like to do and commit yourself to it. Create meaningful action plans to accomplish your dreams. Focus your actions daily on your goals and do something each day that will move you closer to achieving those goals. Plan your work and work your plan. Remain flexible to adapt to changing conditions. Apply the effort to perform the actions necessary to turn your wants into reality. Without this commitment to yourself, you will wind up very frustrated and lament all the things you *could have had,* **if only** you'd acted on your plan.

Beating yourself up for not having taken action on something serves no meaningful purpose. It will only create regrets. Regrets will only make you feel worse and limit your ability to act in the future. If you fail to act on a goal, ask yourself why and what you learned from the experience. Then commit to doing it differently the next time.

Continue learning and looking for opportunities to apply your knowledge and skills. You **will** realize the financial, psychological and emotional rewards you desire. As you evaluate your work and experiences, give yourself credit for what you accomplish. In the end, the person you must please is you. Your conscience will tell you if your actions are consistent with what you want to accomplish.

"The illiterate of the 21st century will not be those who cannot read and write, but those who cannot learn, unlearn, and relearn."
– Alvin Toffler

This poem by Dale Winbrough stresses the importance of being true to yourself [though written in the male gender, the message applies equally to females.]

Man in the Glass

When you get what you want in your struggle for self
And the world makes you king for a day,
Just go to a mirror and look at yourself,
And see what *that* man has to say.
For it isn't your mother or father or wife,
Whose judgement upon you must pass,
The fellow whose verdict counts most in your life,
Is the man staring back from the glass.
Some people may think you're a straight-shooting chum,
And call you a wonderful guy,
But the man in the glass says you're only a bum,
If you can't look him straight in the eye.
He's the fellow to please,
Never mind all the rest,
For he's with you clear up to the end,
And you've passed your most dangerous, difficult test,
If the man in the glass is your friend.
You may fool the whole world
Down your pathway of life
And get pats on your back as you pass,
But your final reward will be heartache and tears,
If you've cheated the man in the glass.

Assuming that your attitude and beliefs are what they should be to open doors of opportunities for you, how will you perform once you find your ideal job? You will most likely be *committed* to performing a job that interests you and provides opportunities for you to use your strengths and abilities and develop skills in an organizational environment whose values are consistent with yours.

In an ideal world, all of these components would be present. In reality, the workplace consists of people whose attitudes, backgrounds, commitment, interests, strengths and values may differ from yours. Surrounded daily by these potential differences can be overwhelming, if you let it. People's expectations will vary regarding what they believe you should accomplish, how you should behave and the quality of work that you should perform. Other people's expectations are based on *their* self-esteem, confidence and fears. Find your own!

You can be and do anything you want in life, as long as you have a plan. Life is what you make it! Grow your dreams, spread your wings, and S O A R!
[Seize Opportunities And Rewards]

TIPS TO SOAR [Seize Opportunities And Rewards]

❖ The ABCs to your success in the workplace and in life are *your*: **A**ttitude, **B**eliefs, and **C**ommitment.

❖ You show commitment to work by consistently showing up each day, doing your job to produce quality work despite other conditions or circumstances in your life.

❖ *Whether you think you can, or you think you can't, you're right.* So, choose to think that you can!

❖ Every work place and life experience is an opportunity to learn. See learning is a life-long process.

❖ Your strategy is like your business plan or road map in life. It tells you where you are headed, what you want to achieve and how you plan to achieve it.

❖ Focus on your goals and do something each day that will move you closer to achieving them.

❖ Plan your work and work your plan

❖ When you lack confidence in your skills and abilities to perform what a job requires, *act 'as if'* you *do* possess these skills.

❖ Your only security in life is to count on your own abilities and efforts to build life-long *employability*.

261

What tips from chapter 12 do *you* value most?
List them below:

Watch out world. Here I come...

SUCCEEDING IN THE WORKPLACE
Critical Skills for a rewarding career and life you love!

ORDER FORM

Quantity	Title	Price	Total
	SUCCEEDING IN THE WORKPLACE Critical Skills for a rewarding career and life you love!	15.95	
	(PA Residents Add 6% Sales Tax)		
	Shipping		
	Amount of Order		

I've enclosed a Check or Money order to Personal Growth Systems or Susan Race.

Name_____

Company or Personal Address_____

City_____ State _____ Zip_____

Phone_____ e-mail_____

Mail to: 553 Aspen Woods Drive * Yardley , PA 19067; 215-493-3325 Fax: 215-493-9363